Teaching

in the

Cracks

Teaching
in the
Cracks

Openings and Opportunities for Student-Centered, Action-Focused Curriculum

BRIAN D. SCHULTZ

Foreword by Deborah Meier
Afterword by William Ayers

TEACHERS COLLEGE PRESS

TEACHERS COLLEGE | COLUMBIA UNIVERSITY
NEW YORK AND LONDON

Published by Teachers College Press, 1234 Amsterdam Avenue, New York, NY 10027

Copyright © 2017 by Brian D. Schultz

Cover by Laura Duffy Design. Cover photo of children by Monkey Business Images; photo of seedling by Evannovostro, both via Shutterstock.

Portions of Chapter 2 are extracted from the unpublished manuscript, "Working toward an alternative: Progressive education in action at The Children's School." Used with the permission of the authors, Brian D. Schultz and Christina Martin.

Portions of Chapter 1 and Chapter 3 are from Schultz, B.D., McSurley, J., & Salguero, M. (2013). Teaching in the cracks: Student engagement through social action currculum projects. *International Journal of Critical Pedagogy, 4*(2), 53–56. Used with permission of the *International Journal of Critical Pedagogy*.

Library of Congress Cataloging-in-Publication Data is available at loc.gov

ISBN 978-0-8077-5831-1 (paper)
ISBN 978-0-8077-7568-4 (ebook)

Printed on acid-free paper
Manufactured in the United States of America

24 23 22 21 20 19 18 17   8 7 6 5 4 3 2 1

For my parents, and Jenn, Keegan, and Addison, with love.

*And, for the educators who are finding openings,
creating opportunities, and imagining possibilities.*

Contents

Foreword

Could there be a topic more important than this one? At this moment in history it's clear that schools should have addressed this topic for all the years in which public education has existed. <u>Our failure to use the years children spend in school to prepare them for the tasks required to maintain democracy, much less nourish it, has injured us deeply.</u>

Regardless of our politics, both the right and the left have deep-seated feelings of estrangement from "their" government. For far too many citizens "the government" seems to belong to someone else, "not us." And as a result, it has been too easy to con them into either not voting or voting against their own interests and preferences. Meanwhile the "con-ers" have used their wealth to influence "our" government. <u>We have become cynics about democracy, and the word itself no longer has the strong appeal it had when I was growing up in the 1930s and 1940s.</u>

The 13-plus years most of us now spend in school hardly touches upon this subject, democracy, that we send young people to die on behalf of! At best one or two civics courses explain how it is supposed to work. And maybe even a little about why. <u>But meanwhile the schools we attend are examples of dictatorships—even if benign ones</u>. The worst crime is noncompliance—insubordination. This goes for principals, teachers, other staff, and children. And this probably is replicated in the central offices that send down the orders. <u>Everyone thinks someone else is in charge.</u>

If we agree that we learn best by doing, as (John Dewey) suggested—and not just listening—then what young people see adults doing is at least as powerful a lesson in organizational life in a democracy as any civics lesson they receive. Demystifying power is in part what a democracy requires us to engage in. <u>Demystifying the power structure</u> of schools might be a good place to start our civics education. <u>With curriculum that students help develop</u>, social action can be a focus and positive change a result.

What is often called service learning—and this book's social action curriculum—gives teachers ways to demystify power. At the schools I was a partner in, like Central Park East Schools in New York City and Mission Hill

※ This is why we need Henrietta LACKs

ix

School in Boston, we asked our students to use their service learning assignments to do just this—to figure out who had power over what, and how it was exercised.

In *Teaching in the Cracks*, Brian Schultz goes further in describing the ways in which the young can become comfortable with their own powers, and how adults can guide them in learning around purpose and into a better understanding of democratic life; both have their joys and responsibilities. Through compelling examples, Brian shares how educators can help students use their powers. The stories he shares are of teachers disrupting the all-too-common top-down approach for an alternative, an alternative that allows students' ideas to guide action, to engage in democratic processes and disagreement, and to make changes in their communities. Engaging students in even one experience where their voices are heard regarding what specific action-directed learning project they will undertake—or, as Brian describes in one example, where they advocate for a more meaningful venue from which their class will graduate—may seem a small start. But such experiences can lead to life-altering changes in how students engage with learning, respect their power to effect change, and see themselves respected by others.

Instead of being afraid of disagreement, of "controversy," our schools must become places that teach us how to disagree, and how to use controversy rather than shy away from it. Democracy is intended as a way to deal with controversy, not a way to eliminate it, or pretend it doesn't exist.

Our fears about opening up such topics, of putting kids into a position where they may be exposed to differences, are well-founded. None of us want our children's schools to "brainwash" them—especially with ideas we disagree with. This tension can't be swept under the rug. Schools must tackle it if they want to really undertake the task that the author is urging them to take on. Like everything else in this important book, it's not going to get easier by postponing it. The time is now.

—*Deborah Meier*

Preface and Acknowledgments

This book has been written as an invitation: An invitation to do something different in classrooms that will not only motivate and engage students, but also show the potential to teach students to be <u>active agents of change in our</u> world. It is about approaching curriculum differently. <u>It is about curriculum</u> <u>as a pursuit of what each student determines to be worthwhile</u>. As practicing and future teachers contemplate the ways that they may involve students in a <u>student-centered</u>, action-focused, and <u>emergent curriculum</u>, my hope is that the practitioners featured in this book—in the multiple contexts of public neighborhood, charter, alternative, and independent schools—will challenge these educators to reflect and rethink practices and personal assumptions. This may enable future teachers to find the openings, the opportunities, and imagine the possibilities to teach in the cracks within our current, broken educational policies.

Due to these <u>constantly shifting mandates</u> and expectations for teachers and students, developing meaningful and worthwhile curriculum has become increasingly difficult. Pressure associated with high-stakes accountability continuously narrows curriculum and limits the <u>ability of teachers to connect</u> <u>with young peop</u>le. But there is hope: <u>A hope that teachers can find ways to</u> <u>develop relevant, responsive curriculum that resonates with the students in</u> <u>their classrooms.</u> *i.e. Henrietta LACKS*

The chapters in this book represent this hopefulness across different grade levels and types of schools. In many of the chapters, I have attempted to make the voices of practitioners prominent either through coauthorship or via extended quotation. I have also shared my writing with each of the practitioners for feedback to ensure that the stories herein accurately represent their perspective. This acknowledges the understanding that should any of them tell the stories themselves, they might have different accounts. Importantly, the practitioners featured in this book are a selected group of educators with whom I have worked in some capacity and who have demonstrated a commitment to teaching in these ways. Each of them brings different perspectives and backgrounds based on their own positionality. My intention is not for readers to consider the aforementioned practitioners or me as an ultimate authority on such curricular approaches, but instead read the ideas as possible ways of thinking about and approaching curriculum in this current moment.

To this end, the book's first chapter lays out a theoretical basis for emergent, democratic, action-centered, and student-led approaches to curriculum. In presenting an argument for developing curriculum that is social action-based and responsive to students' ideas and curiosities, the stage is set for Chapter 2. This chapter, cowritten with a teacher-administrator at a small private progressive school, highlights both the possibilities and complicatedness that occur when honoring children in both design and enactment of an entire school. Because of the curricular freedom afforded at an independent school, readers can see in Chapter 3, which is cowritten with practicing teachers whom I came to know when they were graduate students, that enacting social action curriculum need not be relegated to affluent contexts. In this manner, agency-oriented curriculum flourishes in the classroom of a 1st-year teacher's neighborhood, urban public school. Returning to the independent progressive school, Chapter 4 demonstrates via an interview with a classroom teacher the power of a student-led, problem-oriented curriculum. This interview details a teacher's perspective on how children can follow their interests and become change agents in their school community. In Chapter 5, readers are able to see another view of action-focused curriculum through the partnering of an alternative public high school with community-based organizations to develop democratic educational practice that occurred while working to solve pressing issues in the school's neighborhood. In Chapter 6, teachers in both neighborhood public and public charter schools show how they have found ways to utilize outside educational advocacy organizations committed to social justice and civic engagement to leverage meaningful curricular endeavors with their students amidst a more prescriptive educational context. The book ends with Chapter 7 describing different techniques for democratic participation for the 21st century, detailing various tools as well as organizational resources that promote civic engagement and support teachers. My hope is that the stories throughout the book, coupled with the resources in the final chapter, may guide educators to engage in student-led and action-focused curriculum in their own educational settings.

I am sincerely grateful to the educators whose stories are represented in this book. The work of Elizabeth Hoffman, Will Hudson, Christina Martin, Jennifer McSurley, Matthew Rodríguez, and Milli Salguero inspire me to continue theorizing about curriculum. The work that they do to teach in the cracks is powerful, imaginative, and hopeful. Each of these educators shows me how it is possible to connect with and motivate young people in classrooms through curriculum that emerges from the very questions, ideas, and curiosities that the children name. Thank you, too, to Christy, Jen, and Milli for being wonderful coauthors, and to Will for the great interview.

There are many other people who have contributed to this book in different ways, namely by giving permission to share their images, letters, words, and ideas. Thank you to Nina Allread, Rebecca Atwood, Jill Bass, Jessica Chethik, Teresa Córdova, Tayler Crimaldi, Carlos DeJesús, Katherin Duprey, Elijah Evans, Pamela Freese, Marvin Garcia, Sandra Henkels, Beth-Anne Jacob, Ricardo Jiménez, Laura Ruth Johnson, Samuel Levi Jones, Laura Marquez, Jennifer McSurley and her SVC students and their parents, Laura O'Shea, Matt Peebles, Eileen Rayahin, Ivan Rice, Cathy Schroeder, Devin Sturtevant, Miguel Villareal, Alex Wilson, and any others who I may have left off here or elsewhere in these acknowledgments.

In addition to the educators featured in this book, current and former colleagues in the Goodwin College of Education and Department of Educational Inquiry and Curriculum Studies, as well as my students at Northeastern Illinois University, support and motivate me. Thank you Ken Addison, Sunni Ali, Ann Aviles, Hua Bai, Kimya Barden, Melissa Barone, Sandra Beyda-Lorie, Mike Bochnewych, Anastasia Brelias, Howard Bultinck, Rosetta Cash, Huseyin Colak, MT Garretón, Maureen Gillette, Zada Johnson, Elaine Koffman, Bill Kondellas, Alberto Lopez-Carrasquillo, Jason Lukasik, Kristi Madda, Eleni Makris, Erica Meiners, Linda Nidelkoff, Isaura Pulido, Barbara Quashie, Katy Smith, Lance Williams, Conrad Worrill, and Cate Wycoff. Alison Dover, Tim Duggan, Nicole Holland, Florina Sirb, and Durene Wheeler have really helped me in thinking through parts of this book, for which I am particularly grateful.

Others too acted as a sounding board, provided a platform, taught me to write into the messiness, clarified material, prompted me to theorize about curriculum, and/or wrote generous endorsements: William Ayers, Paris Banks, Lamarius Brewer, Bernard Brommel, Carl Grant, Ming Fang He, Myke Henry, Drew Kemp, Pamela Konkol, Craig Kridel, Sheri Leafgren, Jarred Maddox, Deborah Meier, Rich Milner, Ralph Nader, Pedro Noguera, Kaprice Pruitt, Sarah Reichard, Daniel Ryan, Raynard Thomas, and Kate Van Winkle. And I am especially grateful to William Schubert: His guidance, friendship, and teaching continuously makes me think about curriculum differently, and his ideas related to curriculum theorizing can be seen throughout this book.

Great thanks goes to the wonderful people at Teachers College Press. Jean Ward, your patience, insight, and generous feedback are so highly valued. Carole Saltz, your gentle nudges and suggestions in helping me develop this project are greatly appreciated. Thanks also to Noelle De-La-Paz, Nancy

Power, Jamie Rasmussen, Pete Sclafani, Leyli Shayegan, Lori Tate, and others who have all been a pleasure to work with during the publishing process.

My family is always there for me. Thank you: Mom and David, Dad and Helen, Amy and Chris Soranno, Melani and Kevin Hawkins, Matthew Polk, Grandma Jeanne Wachs, Jim McBride, Lily de Moraes Pissuti, Grazi da Silva Martins, Lindsay Leblang, as well as to my grandparents who are no longer with us. Thanks, too, to my wonderful children, Addison and Keegan. You are constantly teaching me how to be a better dad and I learn so much from you. Your snickers about the title of this book put a smile on my face. My wife Jennifer deserves extra special thanks. Jenn, you are an amazing, patient, tolerant, optimistic wife, mother, and best friend. Your thoughtfulness and your ability to listen and always offer sage advice make me know how grateful, humbled, and excited I am to be on this adventure with you and the kids.

CHAPTER 1

Finding Opportunities and Teaching in the Cracks

There is a fast-changing landscape in education. Schools, teachers, and students continually are adjusting to both rhetoric and mandates that restrict and narrow the very definition of curriculum in classrooms. This reductionary movement in educational policy leads to more and more schooling by traditional methods that often fail to capture the attention of students. High-stakes tests and other pressures associated with the current educational reform movement give critical educators concerned with issues related to justice, equity, and community engagement significant pause. To provide a meaningful curriculum that immerses students in the practice of transferable skills, this group of justice-oriented educators is forced to find ways to teach in alternative and even subversive ways in order to reach the students in their classrooms. Given the climate in schools, teachers and sometimes whole schools must search for and find openings within the mandates or prescriptions in order to "teach in the cracks" of what has been considered the "official curriculum" so that their teaching can connect students with issues relevant to their lives.

These teachers' pedagogy embodies the complexities of teaching. Rather than ignore top-down expectations, a teacher's teach-in-the-cracks process seeks opportunities within or alongside such mandates in order to engage the immediate classroom participants—namely, the students and the teacher working together—in a worthwhile curriculum. Teaching in the cracks addresses an ongoing consternation about having to follow an "expected curriculum" while also promoting discovery and student engagement by placing the students' ideas, interests, and identified community problems at the center of the classroom curriculum. This method leads students to endeavor with their teachers in meaningful curricula both in and outside of the classroom.

This book examines how teachers can find ways to educate in such emergent, democratic ways centered on a progressive educational philosophy that places students' ideas about what is worthwhile as a driving force of what will be studied in the classroom. The stories of educators engaged in this work

1

amid all the high-stakes, troubling, and deficit-oriented rhetoric, and limited interpretations of curriculum, push back on the notion that curricula need to be scripted, teacher-proofed, or exclusively skill-based. Instead, this approach shows the power and potential of teachers exploring with young people to find ways that honor both the curiosities of students and their humanity. In so doing, it encourages opportunities to make schooling experiences responsive to students in what Gloria Ladson-Billings (1995, 2009) has described as culturally relevant ways. Instead of ignoring contextual factors that affect teaching and learning, this approach embraces students as a key component of the curriculum. The schools and teachers highlighted in this book show ways to intrinsically motivate and engage students through approaches to curriculum that lead to more holistic achievement, promote critical thinking and critical understanding, encourage problem posing and problem solving, demonstrate powerful learning, and establish the deep potential for young people to see themselves as active agents in bringing about social change.

LEARNING DEMOCRATIC PROCESSES

Looking to students to generate curriculum serves a significant purpose of education in America, in that it allows students to develop as critical thinkers about real-world concerns. There has long been a premise that schooling in the United States should teach dialogue, deliberation, and debate as a way to encourage and maintain an active democracy. Ideally, such skills are learned within a school curriculum so that competencies are developed and nurtured throughout a child's tenure from preschool through high school. This argument contends that children's experience ought to be steeped in an understanding of and practice in developing democratic communities.

The work of John Dewey frames the need for schools, particularly public ones, to inculcate future generations in learning democratic processes. In his most detailed argument on this idea, *Democracy and Education*, Dewey (1916) contends the "ideal may seem remote of execution, but the democratic ideal of education is a farcical yet tragic delusion except as the ideal more and more dominates our public system of education" (p. 98). In this democratic ideal, schools should be sites that foster students' engagement in decisionmaking, problem solving, and critical thinking. This Deweyan approach to a progressive view of education—where students make decisions, ask questions, solve problems, and actively think, and where content builds upon and emerges from itself—is often in direct contrast with the ways many schools currently function. The norm in schools today has become an overreliance on subject-matter orientations to curriculum, rote learning and memorization of discrete and canonical facts, and attention to results on standardized achievement tests (even when many of the so-called reformers claim that the movement toward Common Core State Standards and their associated tests moves away from this). Dewey (1907) and later Maxine Greene (1986) convincingly promoted schools acting as miniature communities. What would happen if schools were representative of society, as Dewey and Greene argued for, where students learned and practiced teamwork, collaboration, and leadership development through interactions with their peers and teachers each and every day? Such an approach to schooling is not lost among contemporary scholars, although its practices are less often seen in classrooms.

For instance, Pedro Noguera (2003, 2008) challenges us to reflect on and work to reclaim the promise of public education. In his book *City Schools and the American Dream*, Noguera (2003) contemplates hopefulness in imagining a system of schooling that connects with and reaches its students. By drawing on Brazilian educator Paulo Freire's ideas of critical consciousness, reflection, and the need for taking action, Noguera highlights the democratic potential of schools. Importantly, Noguera (2008) poses such a challenge to all of us with students in mind, particularly emphasizing "how listening to students can help schools to improve" (p. 61).

This idea of consciousness can be seen in William Ayers's (2016) book, *Teaching with Conscience in an Imperfect World*. Ayers prompts us to imagine what is possible through schools and schooling:

> Are we conscientiously and systematically teaching free people to participate fully in a free society? In what ways? Could we do a better job of encouraging young people to interrogate the world fully, to ask deeper questions and to pursue those questions to their furthest limits? Do we intentionally and openly help children and youth develop minds of their own? And do we simultaneously offer students opportunities to be responsible and participating members of their communities? What can we imagine our schools being or becoming that they are not yet? How might we get there? (p. 2)

This series of questions likely raises further questions. But imagine, as Ayers encourages us to do, that we took such a deliberation and contemplation to our students. What might the young people believe to be good and just and appropriate for teaching and learning? How can we improve schooling by listening to and learning from students (Noguera, 2008; Schultz, 2011)? It is through such discussions—a miniature community, if you will—that we can not only teach into the cracks of our current system, but also begin to develop a meaningful alternative.

Similarly, William Schubert (2009a) imagines a Utopian alternative world where, building on a John Dewey essay in the *New York Times* from 1933, "there are no schools at all" but instead all sorts of ways to engage in democratic and educational processes. Riffing on Dewey, Schubert, through the first several chapter topics of his book, leads the reader to an imaginary place, a location where education and educational pursuits occur in a multitude of sites: through interactions and gatherings, in assembly places with homelike ambiance, through activities well stocked with resources, and, importantly, where teachers and learners alike learn from one another. Importantly, though, schools like those described by Schubert today and Dewey in 1933 are not common. Undoubtedly, Dewey, Greene, and Freire, and, in turn, Noguera, Ayers, and Schubert, push us to think differently, purposefully, and consciously about how we can create spaces in and out of schools that will enrich and shape young people, ourselves, and our collective communities.

Others, too, have contemplated how we might make good on these ideals in schools today. A significant amount of James Beane's (1993, 1998, 2005) work, for example, is built on Dewey's beliefs and connects to Freirean conceptualizations of critical consciousness. Echoing these ideals, Beane (1993) contends that "[a] curriculum developed apart from the teachers and young people that must live it is grossly undemocratic" (p. 18). If we collectively value such democratic processes in life, Beane argues, then we must nurture such ideals in classrooms to develop students' transferable skill sets. This idea is particularly prominent in Beane's (1993) proposal for a middle school curriculum where, because of their natural development, young adolescents are wrestling with questions about the world and their place within it. This convergence of "who am I in this world" and "what is going on in this world" makes the possibilities endless for classroom topics of study, thematic problems to pose and solve, and activities in which to engage. These opportunities are critical to thinking about teaching in emergent, democratic, and progressive ways: Learning and naming concepts and having opportunities to practice skills in a school setting can be an impetus for students to utilize such transferable knowledge in subsequent classrooms and in their daily lives.

Clearly such an approach to student-centered schooling and learning, where students name topics of interest for study and teachers follow their lead, is not the norm. Authentic problem solving and assessment that embrace such democratic qualities are exceptions in the current climate of standardization. Misguided notions of accountability are antithetical to relevant, responsive approaches to teaching and learning. As a result of current practices, little local control exists and there are seldom any connections to the local context. External expectations from federal policies, state boards of education, or district mandates typically dictate what occurs in classrooms. Teachers are pressured to conform to prescriptive curricula focused on standardized tests; these pressures are underscored by ominous threats of school closings, school turnarounds, and teacher firings. Seldom are teachers' visions of what is possible incorporated into how classrooms evolve or curricula emerge. Added to this already bleak situation, the push for value-added metrics, or what Howard Wainer (2011) has called "uneducated guesses," to measure teacher performance by referencing a teacher's students' test scores highlights such misuse of data to satisfy society's accountability fixation.

The fear tactics, coupled with an often-complacent public, in the name of improving achievement only further an agenda to predetermine, coopt, and restrict curricula. And this agenda occurs despite clear examples of entire countries, such as Finland, that are hopeful and imaginative, and foster low-stakes learning environments while promoting deep engagement (Sahlberg, 2014). This book highlights an alternative that seeks ways to be explicitly student-centered in exploiting cracks and finding openings in a rigid system, challenging the forces undermining the potential of public education. Through democratic, justice-oriented, emergent, and progressive education, there are wondrous possibilities for schooling that honors children and teaches them to be active, politically engaged, justice-oriented citizens.

A FRAMEWORK FOR MAKING IT HAPPEN

How can practitioners realize this theoretical premise for teaching in democratic, justice-oriented, emergent, and progressive ways? A social action curriculum project (SACP) is one approach that offers students opportunities to engage in both democratic processes and experiential learning, while also meeting benchmarks and standards. A SACP focuses classroom activity on the primary concerns of those with the most at stake in the classroom—the students—and constructs spaces and opportunities for them to engage directly in problem solving and agency related to those very concerns. This approach to thinking about curriculum was heavily influenced by my own exposure in the classroom, using the steps associated with and presented in the Center for Civic Education's Project Citizen curricular materials.

Utilizing a SACP framework in the classroom provides teachers with a tool and an approach that are philosophically rooted in the democratic ideals named above and that can lead to creating curricula with their students that are relevant, responsive, and critical within many school settings, including those that are more traditional or restrictive. Through SACPs, teachers can meet district, administrator, and collegial expectations. The SACP can be

viewed as a curricular process that affords teachers and students distinct opportunities to engage in problem posing, problem identification, and problem
solving that center active democratic participation both within and outside
of classrooms. Within these projects are significant hands-on learning opportunities that are authentic since they are neither preconceived nor planned
out in advance. Viewed in this way, SACPs can be seen as an approach to
emergent, action-oriented, project- and problem-based learning that is focused specifically on the named concerns of students. The SACP framework
pushes back against the commonplace curricular approaches that are scripted
and static. As a result, SACPs provide a means to unleash the potential of relevant, responsive curricula that resonate with social issues students encounter
in their daily lives. Thus, a SACP framework can help teachers find openings
within the more "traditional" approaches to teaching and learning and create exciting, enriching, and engaging curriculum that not only captures the
attention of young people but also motivates them to take purposeful action
around their concerns.

So what do teaching and learning look like if we use the students' ideas,
questions, and identified problems as the curricular starting point in the classroom? The reality is that teaching and learning look different in different
settings. This book shows different ways that justice-oriented, democratic
curriculum projects can be enacted in various kinds of schools. Each school
has its own contextual factors and constraints associated with or resisting the
current moment of school reform. Because of this multiplicity, I have shared
examples from diverse school environments, including a K–8 independent
school, a neighborhood public middle school, an alternative public charter
high school, a K–8 public charter school, and a K–8 neighborhood magnet-cluster public school. Each teacher and each school realizes the potential
of utilizing a social action curriculum framework in its own way. My hope is
that readers will reflect on the stories of practitioners in the book and think
about how they might approach this in their own setting with their own
students.

Teaching in the cracks is a way that many teachers or whole schools are
responding to the current moment of school reform. Given the multiplicity
of the kinds of schools that exist in our country today, I show how there are
various ways in which people can respond to this moment and teach in the
cracks. Teaching in the cracks is not a framework or a method per se, but
rather a realization that our current system is not meeting all our students'
needs. It is a realization that we must find ways, by whatever means necessary,
to reach our students. Because context is so critical to how I think about
teaching, learning, and curriculum, I highlight different interpretations of
teaching in the cracks through engaging in democratic, justice-oriented,

emergent, and social action–based curricula in different settings and by different teachers. My hope is to demonstrate that amid all the rigidity, there is the possibility of imagining alternatives. The examples include independent private, neighborhood, charter, and alternative school settings, to show that teaching in the cracks is not limited to a particular group of students from a particular context; instead it is a way to seek the necessary alternative amid the changing landscape that marginalizes students and teachers and inevitably narrows the curriculum.

REFLECTING ON EXPERIENCES

The nexus for this book originates from my ongoing teaching and learning, following my own experiences in the classroom. When I was a teacher in a 5th-grade classroom in a school serving a housing project community, I approached my classroom in a way that I thought might honor what many of the curriculum studies scholars had in mind in their theoretical foundations. I chronicled this approach with one particular classroom in my book, *Spectacular Things Happen Along the Way: Lessons from an Urban Classroom* (2008). For me, approaching classroom curriculum and engagement with students became more important and somewhat intuitive after I initially tried more traditional methods that I was not able to make work well. This is not to say it was easy or that I did not have (constant) angst about whether I was teaching my students well, meeting my students' needs, realizing the best interests of my students, or about whether such a curricular and philosophical approach to the classroom would serve my students in their subsequent years in school. When I write about the intuition to listen to and learn from and with students as a curricular starting point, I neither see this as a sort of received wisdom nor do I want to romanticize it. It was full of rough edges. It was messy. It was complicated. It was complex. But importantly, it was joyful.

Since the time of the classroom journey and its publication in book form, I have grappled with the complexity in showing and teaching about an alternative way of thinking about curriculum. Why do people think that listening to kids is so remarkable? In some ways, it is what education, teaching, and learning should be all about. Looking to students and their concerns, ideas, and imaginations as a natural place for curriculum to begin should be a cornerstone.

My contemplation ends up being something that I bring into my teaching of future and practicing teachers. I often find myself asking students what and how they define curriculum, only to know that I will offer them

Figure 1.1. University students presenting a social action curriculum project centered on the issue of book censorship. (Photo: Brian Schultz)

a different idea. Inevitably the soon-to-be-teachers or those in classrooms readily discuss scope and sequence, standards, and lesson plans. They comment on the rhetoric in the public sphere about what or how schooling is rather than what it should be. And at some level, why shouldn't they? They have become so conditioned—we have become so conditioned—to the notion that this is what curriculum is.

After affirming much of what my students suggest, I offer a nuanced definition, an alternative that potentially encompasses all the things my students name for what may happen in a classroom. But I go further and broader, and more philosophically imaginative, since the alternative definition is not merely for the reasons they mention or to the ends they name. Instead, leaning heavily on the ongoing and influential work of William Schubert (1997; 2009a; 2009b), I suggest that curriculum entails seeking what is worthwhile. (See Figure 1.1 where my students are engaged in a social action curriculum project centered on a topic they determined to be worthwhile). As Schubert (2009b) argues, curriculum can be both content and process that focus on "what is worth knowing, needing, experiencing, doing, being, becoming, sharing, contributing, and wondering?" (p. 22). Building on such a frame, this book is perhaps a distillation of that alternative view of curriculum—a curriculum of what can and ought to be, one that honors and centers young people's ideas of what is worthwhile. What might this look like in action? The practitioners in this book offer some examples that I hope will challenge other educators to pause, reflect, and determine the cracks that they will find, exploit, and teach into in their own teaching practices.

HIGHLIGHTING PRACTITIONERS' PERSPECTIVES

Throughout the book, I have worked to make the voices of educators prominent by coauthoring, interviewing, and using extended quotes from teachers and school administrators so that you as a reader are able to hear directly from educators engaged in this work. The educators in this book embody a hopefulness that surrounds thinking about curriculum differently. As you read about their classrooms and schools, I encourage you to wonder about your own classrooms and your own students' learning. What openings might exist in your school or classroom to teach in the cracks? How would you share authority with your students? How might others respond to this kind of teaching and learning? Imagine what is possible. Dare to journey with your students.

In Chapter 2, I write with Christina Martin, the director of curriculum and instruction as well as a 2nd-grade classroom teacher at The Children's School—a small independent school just outside of Chicago—to lay a theoretical and practical foundation for thinking about democratic and progressive education–based schooling. Together we explore The Children's School as an alternative to the current standards-based trope of schooling in the United States. We frame the school in both a historical and theoretical context to show how its practices and its manifestation of pedagogy can offer intellectual rigor and powerful learning experiences within a community that works to honor each child's individual development and voice. We also outline how the emergent curriculum takes on different forms at different age and grade levels, how the school focuses on authentic assessment and process over product, and what constitutes rigor, while seeking to reclaim this from the neoliberal rhetoric of the moment. We interrogate the privilege and permission to relegate standards to a secondary position behind quality teaching and curriculum that characterize an independent school. Importantly, we utilize the school not as an ideal, but rather as an example of an institution that is striving toward a vision grounded in a Deweyan progressive educational framework and that markedly is operating in the cracks of the broader educational structures associated with mainstream public and private schools.

Questions abound about whether this is possible in other school settings, particularly historically marginalized, public, urban neighborhood schools. These contemplations and questions related to access for democratic, progressive, and emergent curriculum provide an entryway and foundation for

Chapters 3–6. Chapter 3 highlights how Jennifer McSurley, a middle school teacher at an urban neighborhood school, looks to her students for what is worthwhile. The chapter is written with Jennifer, who was a graduate student of mine 8 years earlier, and Milli Salguero, who, at the time of writing the chapter, was my graduate assistant. As Jennifer inverts the curriculum by following the students' ideas and questions through a social action curriculum project, she grapples with the expectations of school administrators and colleagues about what the curriculum is or ought to be, while working to challenge deficit perspectives about her students' capacity. Through Jennifer's narrative storytelling embedded within the chapter, we see one teacher's willingness to find openings to motivate and engage her students. In her classroom, the SACP approach offers students opportunities to engage in both democratic processes and experiential learning, while meeting benchmarks, standards, and outside expectations. It also forces students to negotiate barriers and overcome obstacles that become central to the authentic challenges of emergent curriculum. The chapter demonstrates the possibilities of engaging in emergent, democratic, and progressive education when a teacher, with her students, is willing to search for and find cracks amid the reality of an often-decontextualized curriculum. What is also remarkable about Jennifer's story is her determination to undertake this in her first year of teaching. Whereas many beginning teachers might feel they first should become firmly and safely established, Jennifer felt that she needed to be immediately true to her teaching vision, intentions, and training. She did the work to justify her curriculum and find the cracks within which to teach it. And she and her students reaped the rewards.

Chapter 4 returns to The Children's School to explore the emergent nature of a social action curriculum project through an interview with teacher Will Hudson. In this interview, we are able to visualize, through Will's vivid descriptions, how he nurtured a justice-oriented, integrated curriculum based on the students' curiosities and topical interests related to the broad topic of sickness and death—a topic the students prioritized as one to study. We see how Will both sets up and struggles through a multiple-month-long, comprehensive curriculum that covers subject areas ranging from reading, writing, and social studies to chemistry, physics, and economics. Through this chapter, we hear from a teacher who believes in the power of honoring student voice. Will demonstrates the operation of an open teaching mind that balances an understanding of how students might be helped to most fully realize learning and social action objectives with respect for their authority as creators, designers, and elaborators of their own learning.

In Chapter 5, I look to an alternative high school in Chicago that also delves deep into powerful democratic and social justice–based curriculum with students and the community. The Dr. Pedro Albizu Campos Puerto Rican High School (PACHS) approaches emergent curriculum from a different angle. Instead of looking to the students—many of whom were either pushed out or dropped out of the neighborhood schools—to name topics they deem worthwhile, the teachers and school administrators partner with and invite community organizations to look to the students to help solve problems in the community. PACHS shows how a school can frame a pedagogical intent for students to use their voices in purposeful ways to speak out about and take action on community issues that are real and relevant. Students are afforded firsthand opportunities to make a difference in the community by working with local organizations that partner with the school in what is called the Sustainable Democracy Project. The vision and practices of teacher Elizabeth Hoffman and principal Matthew Rodríguez demonstrate the potential of fostering a curricular approach that harnesses student interest while serving the community and promoting agency.

Chapter 6 focuses on teachers Milli Salguero and Jennifer McSurley—the coauthors of Chapter 3—by highlighting their work as they lean heavily on outside organizations to teach in ways they feel will resonate with their students. The chapter details how Milli, a teacher at a K–8 public charter school, wants to be a progressive, democratic, and justice-oriented teacher who engages in robust and emergent social action curriculum projects, but admittedly, given her and her school's interpretations of outside mandates, is in a struggle to become the teacher she envisions. This chapter shows that even in more restrictive environments resulting from district policies, there are still possibilities for both Milli and her students to engage in justice-oriented work. Although Milli is not yet the teacher she wants to be, she accomplishes an inquiry-based, justice-oriented curriculum by working with educational organizations, such as Facing History and Ourselves, that provide standards-aligned resources and professional development to teachers who are interested in connecting their classrooms and the curriculum in culturally relevant and responsive ways. Likewise, I look to Jennifer's classroom, in a neighborhood magnet-cluster K–8 public school, to show how she finds opportunities to develop projects with students based on issues they name as important. Now an experienced teacher who used social action curriculum projects in another school, Jennifer does this by utilizing district partnerships and curricular frameworks offered by the organization Mikva Challenge. Both teachers are presented in the context of a misinterpretation or misuse of the Tyler Rationale, a common approach to curriculum and instruction used in many schools today. Taken together, these teachers provide readers with examples of ways to connect with students through justice-oriented curriculum in environments where it may not seem possible.

Chapter 7 focuses on ways to take action that are demonstrated within the previous chapters in what Katherine Isaac (1992, 1997) calls "techniques for participation." Teachers in this book and others with whom I have worked often wonder about how to take the proverbial turn to getting their students to engage in action. As a classroom teacher and now as a college professor, I was inspired by Isaac's analysis of techniques for participation related to multiple civil rights movements over the 20th century. This chapter highlights some of the techniques that have given my college students guidance, ideas, and direction for taking action. Since the methods for taking action are somewhat dated, given the advent of social media and the Internet in the 21st century, I offer some ideas and perspectives on more current techniques of participation, to assist teachers in engaging in action-oriented, emergent curricula with their students. In addition, I point to some organizations and resources that champion engaged and social justice–oriented curriculum that also may assist teachers.

Collectively, the chapters in the book are intended to challenge readers to think about what is possible. To imagine a different kind of curriculum. To rethink their assumptions. To search for the opportunities so they might find ways to teach that honor the interests of the children in their classrooms and that will promote a more just society and an enriching, engaging school experience.

CHAPTER 2

Working Toward an Alternative
Progressive Education in Action

with Christina E. Martin

Defining progressive education is complex. Explanations of how the term *progressive education* came into being, the reasons for the progressive education movement itself, and the actual practices of progressive education continue to create heated debates today as they have over the past 125 years. As Lawrence Cremin (1961) argued in his acclaimed historical account of progressive education, *The Transformation of the School*, there is no "capsule definition" (p. x). What is agreed upon, however, is that the naming of a different kind of education in opposition to the traditional approach came into fashion during what has been called the progressive era of the United States, a period in which the country was undergoing spectacular social, economic, and political changes.

During this time, a confluence of several key factors perpetuated a need for a different approach—one that would meet the needs of a new, more industrialized society—to public education. The country was in the midst of tremendous change, with populations increasingly moving toward cities and away from more rural settings. A shift to manufacturing created a class of unionized, often low- or de-skilled, workers (see, for example, Oakes, Lipton, Anderson, & Stillman, 2012). Coupled with historically high rates of immigration, these factors spurred what was deemed a necessary change in the American approach to schooling. Different manifestations of progressive education became alternatives to how teaching and learning had been conceptualized and practiced previously in the United States.

At its core, progressive education was a rejection of what came before. The classical, traditional curriculum, focusing as it did on rote memorization within each subject area, was seen as insufficient to meet the needs of a changing society. A different way of educating the masses through compulsory schooling could help to solve many societal issues. For instance, progressive schooling could ameliorate the problems of high dropout and juvenile delinquency rates caused by disinterested, unmotivated students (Cremin, 1961). Similarly, progressive schooling could mitigate the effects of immigration by creating a "shared" American educational experience. Finally, progressive schooling could help society shift away from subjective religious doctrine and toward objective scientific truth, as called for in the political and philosophical thinking of the day.

The progressive movement, an attempt to solve those and other problems, began in the late 1800s. In 1919 the Progressive Education Association (PEA) was formed to perpetuate a shared understanding of how to best combat the problems of the nation's schools. Although, according to Cremin, the PEA was originally a somewhat marginal organization, it developed a statement of principles that could guide the overarching ideas of those in teachers' colleges and those simply interested in helping to change the way that education was enacted with children. The ideals in the PEA's statement included freedom to develop naturally, interest as a motivating factor in work, teacher as guide not taskmaster, scientific study of pupil development, more attention to child physical development, cooperation between home and school, and the progressive school as a leader in education movements (Association for the Advancement of Progressive Education, in Cremin, 1961). Steve Tozer and Guy Senese (2012) interpret the movement as having key common assumptions about what progressive education meant at the time, which continue to this day: (1) curriculum is activity-based rather than focused on memorization and rote learning; (2) schooling and curriculum should reflect the needs and the interests of the children in the classroom; (3) schooling should reflect society; and (4) in turn, schooling should work to solve society's problems.

Despite general agreement on these principles, both during the progressive era and today, interpretations of them can vary widely. Tom Little and Katherine Ellison's book, *Loving Learning: How Progressive Education Can Save America's Schools* (2015), highlights these differences based on Little's cross-country tour of some 45 schools. From various interactions and interviews with many progressive educators, Little synthesized a characterization of progressive education, pushing back against Cremin's assertion that there was no capsule definition: "Progressive Education prepares students for active participation in a democratic society, in the context of a child-centered environment, and with an enduring commitment to social justice" (p. 52). In 2016, the Progressive Education Network (PEN), an organization that links its history to the PEA and articulates "principles of progressive education" for individual educators and member schools to emulate, took Little's assertion about the "enduring commitment to social justice" to the next level. Refining its guidelines, PEN (2016) calls for a progressive education inextricably linked to racial justice where "education must amplify students' voice, agency, conscience, and intellect to create a more equitable, just, and sustainable world."

Both Little's justice-oriented definition of progressive education and PEN's call for racial justice within progressive education are significant, considering that an early interpretation of progressive education, that was parallel to Tozer and Senese's (2012) four tenets, was to sort children based on their purported capabilities that were race-, class-, and gender-based. Depending on his or her "stock," each child had a place in society, and it was the school's role to groom children for their appropriate place. Influenced greatly by the emerging scientific management theories of the day championed by Frederick Winslow Taylor (1911) and his effort to develop "the one best way" (Kanigel, 1997), this manifestation of progressive education was activity-based and interest-based, reflective of society and committed to solving society's problems, but without much input from the students themselves or their parents. In other words, the "interests" and "needs" of the child were determined primarily by external decisionmakers. Another interpretation, in line with the stances of Little and PEN, in which the student contributes information about his or her own interests and needs, presents a wholly different approach to teaching and learning.

This latter interpretation of progressive education, coupled with the need for an education that is justice-oriented, is where we situate our thinking. Influenced greatly by the works of John Dewey, this view of progressive education takes the child as the centerpiece of the curriculum. The focus on experiential learning, reflection of society, and working toward solving society's problems stems from Dewey's (1907) ideal that schools were to be embryonic communities where democratic living was taught and practiced. Later Dewey (1938) argued convincingly that the experiences (and in turn the interests) of the child could be a starting point for the curriculum in school and gradually would build to encompass learning in all disciplines of knowledge and subject areas. It was the deliberate role of the teacher to make sure that content was both taught and covered through the natural curiosities of young people. Content seldom was taught in isolation or for its own sake, but instead was interwoven and interconnected to help children connect school material to their lives at the moment. Progressive education in this way looked to students as experts in their own lives and stakeholders in their own learning.

Importantly, though, this view of education does not merely follow the whim of the child. Children's identification of their own interests and needs demonstrates their keen desire and ability to make sense of the world around them, and to take action to understand the world and make it a better place.

As William Schubert (2012), building on Dewey's theorizing, contends:

> The heart and soul of progressive education is much more than simple catering
> to the surface interests of children; rather, progressive education taps the pow-
> erful desire of every human being to imagine and create meaningful lives. We all
> wonder what is worth wanting, knowing, experiencing, doing, being, becoming,
> overcoming, sharing, and contributing. Children are no exception to such won-
> dering, questioning, and constructing who they are. It is reflected in the essence
> of their play which is their serious and joyful work. (p. 4)

CONTEMPORARY ANTI-PROGRESSIVE PRESSURE

In 2013 remarks to the American Society of News Editors, then-U.S. Secretary of Education Arne Duncan stated, "What our young people need, and
deserve, is an education that leaves them not just college-ready but innovation-ready" (para. 13). At face value, Duncan's rhetoric is intriguing. Few
would disagree that our children *need* learning opportunities that promote
innovation, engagement, and problem solving. Our children *deserve* spaces in
school to nurture creativity and develop critical thinking. But Duncan's call
to action begged many questions about what is meant by innovation-ready
and how American schooling can foster such a lofty goal.

Despite purporting to provide an answer to the "crisis of low standards"
through "the power of the Common Core [State Standards (CCSS)]," Duncan's speech was nothing new. The CCSS attempt to create a national curriculum based on rigor, high expectations, and competitiveness through a standardized set of learning goals and objectives. Far from providing an answer
to current educational woes, the CCSS continue the educational policies that
have become commonplace for the past decade and a half under No Child
Left Behind (2001) and Race to the Top (2009), where educational success
is measured through children's performance on high-stakes testing designed
by big-house publishing companies.

As educators have learned, it is extremely difficult to argue for "leaving
children behind" or not participating in the "race to the top." Examples of
authentic innovation in the classroom are harder and harder to come by,
primarily because the national education policies force an approach that con-
trols educational discourse and classroom practices about how children learn,
how students are viewed in and out of school, and how both students and
teachers are evaluated. An overreliance on standardized test scores and the
advent of value-added metrics place the focus on children's shortcomings
and reduce complex individuals—both students and teachers—to their test

performances. These views often miss the opportunity to frame schooling as a means of possibility, potential, and developing the capacity of young people. And, unfortunately with the recent appointment of Betsy DeVos as the U.S. Secretary of Education—a proponent of school vouchers, increasing charter schools options, and other means of privatizing public education—we are likely to see more of the same, without wholesale changes to educational policy. But are there viable alternatives and, if so, what do they look like?

AN APPROACH FOR RESISTING SCHOOLING AS USUAL

One alternative approach to this corporatized model of "innovation" is a school that champions its mission in the historical ideals of progressive education and in the practices of developing democratic schools. This approach centers the school as an incubator for democracy. It works to develop community among all its constituents along with curriculum that is integrative, fluid, and emergent. It looks to its teachers and students as co-creators and designers of the school's curriculum. And it believes that evaluation and assessment can be integrated into learning and used to identify strengths as well as weaknesses as part of an ongoing process of reflective growth. This alternative approach challenges much of the current thinking regarding what is and is not possible in schools today.

The Children's School

This chapter highlights this alternative schooling approach, an approach nested in a democratic, progressive vision for education. This vision, respecting teachers as experts in education, striving to honor the full humanity of children, and encouraging young people to express themselves in order to solve authentic problems, has deep potential to challenge the marketplace ideas touted by former Secretary Duncan, Secretary DeVos, and others. We take a close look in this chapter at The Children's School (TCS)—a small, independent school just outside of Chicago—as a specific example of a different approach to curriculum, teaching, and learning. TCS is working to resist the notion that outside policymakers know what is best for its students and teachers. It attempts to offer intellectual rigor, challenging curriculum, and engaging learning experiences, while listening to and learning from children. The TCS model provides a stark contrast to current educational practice as dictated by the CCSS and associated efforts.

This chapter is written from a vantage point close to the school. Both Christina, my coauthor, and I have been closely connected over time to TCS.

Both of us are members of the school's board of directors, Christina is the school's director of curriculum and instruction, she teaches 2nd grade at the school, and her daughter is a school alumna. I currently am a parent of two children at the school and see many curricular enactments at TCS as examples of the principles I propound as a university professor who teaches about progressive education and democratic schools.

We use three basic components of progressive education—democratic community practices; emergent curriculum and play- , project- , and problem-based learning; and authentic assessment and process over product—to demonstrate how one particular school places student voice at the center of its pedagogy. While we offer TCS as a viable example of progressive education and as an alternative to market-driven reform models, we want to be careful not to romanticize TCS. Our goal rather is to highlight that as a society we may indeed work toward alternatives that honor and challenge teachers and students alike to engage in meaningful and worthwhile learning. The school operates from a position that this effort is a collective one; that it is complicated, complex, and hardly simple; and that there are often many rough edges as the school seeks to create learning spaces that are consistent with its beliefs and in line with its mission. We also recognize that since TCS is a private tuition-funded school, its students come from families that have an option to pursue alternative choices in their children's educational experiences. Further, because the school has limited scholarship funds, there are also very few students of material poverty, a condition associated with a constellation of challenges to learning. Historically, progressive education often has been associated with the education of more affluent students or with schools that serve more affluent communities. Although there are examples of progressive education serving students in historically marginalized communities, it is necessary to point out the very real issues related to student access and the limiting nature of this pedagogical approach for students who may not have the socioeconomic means to attend a private school or to move to an area served by a progressive public school.

What Makes The Children's School Unique?

TCS was founded in 2004 by Daniel P. Ryan as an independent, progressive K–5 elementary school. The school began with 13 students in kindergarten and 1st grade. By its 3rd year, TCS had grown to 40 students, and current enrollment is over 100 students. In 2013, TCS expanded to include grades 6 through 8. From kindergarten through 8th grade, TCS teachers and students implement an emergent curriculum based on experiential, inquiry- and project/problem-based learning, along with a strong democratic decision-making component.

True to its progressive and democratic ideals, the pedagogy at TCS has as its cornerstone the honoring of children's voices (Ryan, 2017). This means that children, the primary stakeholders in any system of education, have a substantial say in both the academic and operational aspects of the school. This type of learning community is messy, chaotic, and difficult, and also powerful, nurturing, and rewarding.

LIVING DEMOCRATIC PRACTICES

If schools are to be places that actively promote and practice democracy as a way of defining a culture, a way of living together, and a way of communicating, how exactly should that be enacted? As detailed in Little and Ellison's (2015) book, there are many schools across the country that are trying to make good on school as a means to promote and practice democracy. These include notable public examples like Winnetka Public Schools north of Chicago and Mission Hill School in Boston, and private schools such as Park Day School in Oakland, California, and Wingra School in Madison, Wisconsin. TCS is not alone in this quest, and the school has been influenced in attempts at answering this question not only by John Dewey, but also by Paulo Freire's (2000) notion of problem posing, and by the examples of other schools that are trying to enact progressive education. All share the philosophy that those who have the most at stake must be able to use their voices in purposeful ways to affect the decisionmaking, governance, and implementation of curriculum. As Deborah Meier, the pathbreaking founder of progressive public schools including the Central Park East schools and Mission Hill School, contends, within a democratic school "you're continuously exploring how everybody's voice can be heard, and acted upon, effectively" (in Knoester, 2012, p. 12).

At TCS, children are full-fledged members of the school community, expected to uphold the rights and responsibilities of community membership, and valued for their talents, ideas, and opinions. This is easy to say but, in our experience, rare to practice on an institutional level. Many adults do not seem to fully believe that children have ideas or opinions as good or as valid as those of adults. Certainly, adults have more experience in the world, along with the broader perspective such experience brings. However, children do, of course, have many excellent ideas and opinions—perhaps in part because they are not as hampered as adults by conventional wisdom, contextual constraints, or a sense of what "has been" or "should be" done. Teachers at TCS are comfortable saying, "Well, I'm not sure what we should do about (a particular topic), but let's bring it to Town Hall Meeting and see if anyone has any great ideas."

At the classroom level, formal democracy takes the form of a weekly Group Meeting. Students take turns leading this meeting, following an agenda that has been set through a sign-up sheet on which children or teachers can list topics for discussion. In a 2nd-grade classroom, for example, a typical agenda item might be "using too many blocks." The child bringing up the topic explains briefly what the problem is—some children (no names are used) use so many blocks during choice time that there are not enough for the rest of the children who wish to build. Discussion ensues, moderated by the child leading the meeting, with help from the teacher as needed. The deliberation is solution-focused, and after several ideas have been offered, there might be a vote if no consensus emerges.

If the previous paragraph makes the Group Meeting sound simple or easy, it isn't. Many times, issues are difficult to talk about and difficult to solve. Some issues cannot be definitively "solved" at all, but rather remain a problem the class works on throughout the entire school year. For teachers, the Group Meeting requires time and energy. Children need one-on-one support to articulate their concerns and handle their emotions in productive ways. And committing the time and resources to a robust Group Meeting necessarily means taking time away from something else in the curriculum.

Separate from Group Meetings, the entire TCS community gathers weekly for a Town Hall Meeting. This again is led by a student—typically an older student because it calls for some fairly well-developed skills to manage a meeting this large. A sign-up sheet for agenda items is used, and students are encouraged to sign up when their concern has been discussed at the classroom level but requires further discussion or action by the entire school. Topics often include things like: "washing hands after recess"—too many people trying to wash hands all at once or "recess before lunch"—a preference over the school's old schedule, which was lunch before recess. Sometimes the topic is an idea for a fun event, such as a dance party or all-school pajama day. Town Hall Meetings, like classroom ones, focus on solutions and also may culminate in a vote.

In the hand-washing traffic jam example above, students decided to implement a system of bathroom monitors—one boy and one girl each day— who would stand at the bathroom doorways to allow only a few children to enter at a time. The 5th-graders agreed to take on this task. Over the ensuing weeks, this same topic was reintroduced several times. This is a frequent occurrence, and part of what TCS is trying to foster—a willingness to try out a solution, assess its effectiveness, and return to the group for modification if necessary. At one point the modification required was simply to remind all members of the community to respect the bathroom monitor's authority and wait to enter the bathroom until given the OK. At another point, a younger child asked why only 5th-graders were allowed to be bathroom monitors, and eventually this resulted in all grade levels, including kindergartners, taking on the responsibility of bathroom monitoring for some period of time.

There is one other notable aspect of the voting process at TCS. The final question, after the majority has spoken and one idea or solution has prevailed, is for the minority voters: Can you live with it? At this point, people who did not vote for the winning idea are invited to offer a compelling reason why the majority should change its mind. This happens rarely, because often the person who "can't live with it" offers some version of "I don't agree" and gives reasons that have already been debated. However, in one famous incident, after a vote to allow nuts in classrooms in which there were no allergic students, but not to allow nuts in classrooms with one or more allergic students, the majority was persuaded to change its mind. In response to, "Can you live with it?" a kindergarten child raised his hand and said he couldn't live with it because he himself had a nut allergy, and the new rule meant that he could not eat lunch in any classroom but his own (thus missing out on the highly popular weekly all-school lunch in which children may choose any classroom and go there to eat lunch). An audible gasp was heard as children realized the unfairness of the situation, and a re-vote was taken, making all classrooms nut free.

These are some of the highlights of Town Hall Meetings over the years at TCS. On any given day, a Town Hall Meeting might be tedious, repetitive, or frustrating. A few years ago, teachers had to make a decision about how much time and energy to commit to Town Hall Meetings, and more recently have had to revisit whether the entire school should be present or whether it is more appropriate to separate the middle-level grades from the elementary ones because of topics of interest or necessity based on student ages. Teachers were finding that if there was nothing listed on the agenda, and no big item that faculty wanted to discuss, it was easy to skip a meeting here and there in favor of a fieldtrip or an art activity. Sometimes TCS would go a month or longer without one. Then teachers began to see that students, particularly the younger students, weren't learning the routines and skills of an effective Town Hall Meeting. Teachers decided to recommit to holding the meetings regularly; the routine practice of democratic processes, even if each and every session is not groundbreakingly important, is vital in order to have the structure in place when a challenging issue does arise for the community.

The Town Hall Meeting decisionmaking process mirrors the faculty decisionmaking process. Since the faculty is a small group of 10–12 teachers, there is rarely a formal vote, but most programming and curricular decisions are reached by consensus after discussion. In addition, faculty actively work on being willing to try something—whether a new curricular initiative or a solution to a particular problem—and then change and try something else if the original idea is not working. Again, while this approach is rich and deeply rewarding as a work environment, it is not without tension and struggle at times. Overall, the faculty believe that the tension and struggle are a necessary part of creating a community that engages in dialogue and group decisionmaking.

EMERGENT CURRICULUM AND PLAY-, PROJECT-, AND PROBLEM-BASED LEARNING

Because TCS has created a space where participants—from teachers and administrators to students and parents—use their voices in purposeful ways, an emergent curriculum centered on issues relevant to the students themselves can unfold. The power of this emergent approach derives from addressing the explicit needs and interests of the immediate stakeholders in a cooperative space that centers on personal growth rather than a top-down manner (Hopkins, 1954). We are reminded of William Ayers's (2011) assertion that within the interconnectedness of a progressive curriculum, "you can learn everything from anything" (p. 96). Rather than a static list of skills and concepts organized by discipline to be mastered at each grade level, emergent curriculum arises directly from the children. It is the role of the teacher to weave traditional skills and concepts associated with reading, writing, math, social studies, and science into the larger topics or projects brought forth by the children. In this way, the curriculum allows spaces, opportunities, and challenges for students to think, engage, question, and act.

Evidence of student interests driving curriculum are found in each classroom at TCS. In the kindergarten room, for example, a large chicken wire "Maisasaura nest" was created one year when several children were seen to share an interest in dinosaurs. In 3rd grade, children's elaborate dioramas—created during choice time after the teacher read aloud *The Last of the Really Great Whangdoodles*—are given space in the classroom and time on the daily schedule. In 6th grade, students are given space—both physical and digital—to post ideas, jokes, pictures, and other materials that they find interesting. This informal, open sharing of ideas can lead, for example, to one student's fascination with reptiles sparking a months-long project engineering and building a new stand that could hold a 150-gallon tank for the classroom's spotted turtles.

Once students have a topic they wish to pursue—such as animals, space, or Egypt—the project begins to unfold (see Figure 2.1). Students and teachers may decide to hatch chicks in the classroom, build the International Space Station and role-play being astronauts, or mummify a chicken and bury it in a tomb created in the cloakroom. Children are engaged, active, conducting research to find out what needs to be created, and then doing the actual work of creating it—whether "it" is written instructions for the care of chicks, wearable space suits for the astronauts, or tomb paintings and relics for "King Cluck." The curriculum becomes a living, breathing creation of the ongoing learning community, generating great excitement about academics and school in general among teachers and students alike.

At other times, a teacher might notice a particular interest among students and use that to initiate a project. For example, a 1st-grade teacher at TCS noticed that her students frequently were putting on "shows" for one another during choice time—acting out stories, wearing costumes, handing out tickets to prospective audience members. The teacher decided, with the children's approval, to make theater the topic of study in the classroom for the next several weeks. Students visited a local theater and took a backstage tour, researched various topics (e.g., how does a fly system work?), and worked together to write and produce their own plays, which they then shared with the rest of the school community. In the meantime, they also explored simple machines associated with the fly system, and mathematical concepts of area, perimeter, addition, and multiplication as they designed and sewed a curtain for their stage out of 12" x 12" squares of fabric.

TCS works to interpret its emergent, progressive curriculum across the grade levels on a continuum, moving from play-based to project-based to problem-based as children mature, while making sure that students are taught and develop skills so as to progress along this continuum. Young children explore the world through play and do not distinguish between play and learning. TCS agrees with Vivian Paley's (2005) contention that play for young children is serious work. For example, when a kindergarten child is building a block structure, is she playing, or exploring rudimentary physics principles? The school takes children's curiosity about the world as the starting point for curriculum. Thus, progressive teaching for young children is play-based, guided by children's innate desire to make sense of the world around them and to engage with the world through play.

At the same time, however, not all learning at TCS takes place explicitly through play. Instruction in reading and math, to give two examples, is not entirely play-based. Teachers may seize opportunities that emerge through play and are encouraged to do so, but do not wait to introduce topics in reading and math until they arise in children's play. Teachers will not only look

Figure 2.1. A 2nd-grade student works with duct-tape and cardboard to build a replica ship based on a classroom project and study of the *Titanic*. (Photo: Brian Schultz)

Figure 2.2. A 5th-grader explores the globe in a claw-foot bathtub under a student-designed classroom loft. (Photo: Brian Schultz)

for opportunities to tie academic subjects to student interests, but also design instruction to bring developmentally appropriate academic skills and topics to children. For instance, reading is taught in play-based contexts and in multifaceted ways that include independent reading, both whole- and small-group phonemic awareness, read-alouds, book groups, research-oriented reading, and a writing program that has children from kindergarten through 8th grade engaged in the writing process. This writing process helps to teach reading as students develop skills from drafting and editing to illustrating and publishing their work. Likewise in math, students are taught numeracy skills and mathematical concepts in ways that arise out of children's play as well as through planned curricula designed by teachers.

While teachers move between a play-based learning environment and one that deliberately scaffolds, plans, and teaches specific skills, children's voices and initiative are honored as they choose materials to read, topics to research, and stories to write. Teachers support children in developing interests and curiosity to guide their learning in a low-pressure environment, particularly around reading acquisition (see Figure 2.2). This is in stark contrast to many norms in other schools where students who do not reach specific reading benchmarks at each grade level are deemed as deficient or "behind" and singled out for remediation.

In the middle and late elementary years, the curriculum shifts away from a purely play-based approach to a project-based one. As children gain more skills and modalities for engaging in inquiry and discourse, the need for a large portion of the curriculum to be approached through play becomes diminished. Project-based learning may still involve a significant element of play, of course, as children explore topics and take on roles or personas within the topic area in order to deepen their understandings. As children progress developmentally within the project-based environment, the role of the teacher is critical, guiding and facilitating learning while also ensuring that specific skills and content are both covered and taught within context. (For a treatment of important factors related to project-based learning, see, for example, Larmer & Mergendoller, 2010.)

By the time children reach early adolescence, the curriculum shifts once again to accommodate their changing developmental needs, from a strictly project-based to a more problem-based approach (see Figure 2.3). Problem-based curriculum asks students to identify problems, concerns, and questions about the world and then work with their teachers to craft responses. This approach is in line with James Beane's (2005) work on finding the intersection between students' personal concerns or questions and those relating to the larger world. For example, young adolescents may have questions about their own identities and how they fit in with their peer groups; this can be connected to larger social questions about how entire groups identify themselves and find their place in a society (e.g., immigrants or minority groups). Or, a question about personal health and body image could be related to food safety and the global allocation of food resources. In this way, adolescents' views are expanded and enriched, even as the curriculum addresses the more narrow and self-interested concerns of the typical adolescent. As the students begin to read the world and determine their places within it, a problem-based, problem-posing curriculum becomes a powerful vehicle for making meaning about themselves and their places in the world (Ayers, 2004; Freire, 2000).

One of the great advantages of project work is that it can be implemented on a very individual basis. In a traditional, standards-based classroom, differentiation requires layers of planning and organization and often takes the form of handing students a different, harder worksheet or task once they complete the initial worksheet or task. But in TCS's project-based approach, differentiation occurs more organically as students choose individual topics to research and individual tasks to complete. There is not an attempt to have every student working on the same skill at the exact same time, because teachers understand that each child is at a unique place in his or her development, and is ready for particular skills and concepts that build on what he or

Figure 2.3 Students examine and research information on contemporary social justice issues. (Photo: Brian Schultz)

she already knows and understands. Instead of competing with one another to finish first, to read the hardest book, or to get the highest grade, children at TCS learn to rely on one another and themselves for their unique talents and abilities, and also to ask for help and collaborate with others to create something bigger and better than they could create alone. Whereas framing this idea is powerful in its own right, how the school and teachers react to notions of readiness for skills and content is complex, and as a result has the potential to sometimes miss the mark. Students can become complacent in such an environment, and students with learning needs beyond the scope of the classroom teachers' skill set or training have to be addressed. Teachers need to get to know their students very well and have to become readily familiar with individual students' comfort zones so as to challenge and push them, and also recognize when and what may be needed if a child is not progressing in a developmentally appropriate way.

AUTHENTIC ASSESSMENT AND PROCESS OVER PRODUCT

Teachers at TCS take a view of assessment that stands in stark contrast to the one promulgated by proponents of high-stakes standardized testing. Indeed, many progressive schools rarely "test" children, at least in the traditional sense of the word. Progressive schools instead rely on other ways to evaluate children's growth, including formally or informally evaluating authentic artifacts of student learning, looking at the whole child as a complex individual with both strengths and challenges, and guiding children (and their parents) to engage in their own goal-setting and reflective processes (see Darling-Hammond, Ancess, & Falk, 1995; Janesick, 2006).

Progressive educators seek to integrate assessment into children's learning rather than having assessment be a separate event after the learning has taken place. This type of teaching focuses on means rather than ends, as Dewey argued for in *The School and Society* (1907), and avoids a mere collection of facts, principles, or skills. With so many facts, formulas, and figures at our technology-connected fingertips, it is more imperative than ever that students focus on the process of applying knowledge and evaluating claims or sources, rather than on simple recall, rote performance of skills, or the creation of some arbitrary product.

By looking at the whole child as a complex individual, rather than a checklist of skills or concepts that either have or have not been mastered, progressive teachers do not view their primary job as identifying and correcting each child's deficits. With the understanding that all human beings have things they struggle with or find difficult, the teacher's goal is to help children recognize and improve in areas of challenge, whether academic or social–emotional, while also helping them build on their unique talents and strengths.

At TCS, students, parents, and teachers work collaboratively to set goals for each child at the beginning of the academic year. Midyear brings a second parent–teacher–student conference (45 minutes to an hour in length) accompanied by a narrative report documenting the student's academic and social–emotional growth during the year so far. At year's end, a final conference has all stakeholders looking back on the goals set in September and reflecting on what progress was made toward them. No grades are given and children are not compared with one another. Instead, teachers look for growth along a child's own unique developmental arc and document this formally through a narrative report card. Students' own insights and reflections about what they want to achieve and how they want to achieve it are treated as valuable; indeed, in some respects, those individual goals drive the entire assessment process. Narrative report writing has its challenges. It is time-consuming. It can push teachers to the point of exhaustion. It can miss the nuances of an individual, albeit less so than grades. Narrative reports also force parents to see markers of progress and achievement differently than the more traditional accounting of student grades. Narrative reports are not so different from traditional report cards in that teachers and their students have a lot at stake in such snapshot reporting. The accuracy of an assessment of a student's progress can "make or break" how the child sees him- or herself in a particular area of academics or socioemotional development. Because the reporting is interpretive by its very nature, teachers have a lot of pressure to "get it right."

Progressive schools, and TCS is no exception, have long struggled with the criticism that the focus on democratic processes and social–emotional issues, along with the lack of a "set" curriculum and formal assessment, indicates a lack of rigor in the academic program. Parents may worry that their children will not be ready for high school, or college, or their eventual career. This is a constant source of tension in many progressive communities, as parents may advocate for more standardization in curricular content or assessment based on their perception of what their children "need" to succeed in later endeavors. At TCS, for example, middle-level faculty initially grappled with how to handle students who might require grades in order to apply to selective high schools. Should TCS assign those children grades instead of, or in addition to, the narrative reports? If so, what should those grades be based on? Would this compromise the school's progressive ideals, or be aligned with them?

THE RHETORIC OF RIGOR AND NEED TO KEEP PUSHING TOWARD JUSTICE

As an attempt at a present-day embodiment of democratic ideals, progressive education broadly and TCS in particular work to provide an alternative to the current educational approach of high-stakes testing, college and career readiness, and standards-based curriculum. This democratic approach challenges some common uses of "rigor" that are associated with perceived abilities in which standardized test scores serve as a proxy for sorting children, often inherently based on race and socioeconomic class. Reminiscent of some early interpretations of race-, class-, and gender-based progressive education, democratic-oriented progressive educators now need to assertively enter the national debate about rigor in order for this schooling approach to gain traction in the broader educational community.

Further, progressive educators must not only show the power of teaching and learning through these means, but also internalize and actualize critical components of teaching for racial and socioeconomic justice as a key component of their work. By redefining rigor as learning that is deep, rich, and critical, and learners as thoughtful, thorough, and conscientious, progressive educators can strike back against the current educational landscape that defines rigor by the number of facts learned, number of tests taken, or quantifiable levels of achievement and aptitude. Instead, a rigorous curriculum should be conceived as one that promotes certain habits of mind, such as critical thinking, asking "why?", creative problem solving and problem posing, finding and evaluating sources of information, and building a capacity for empathy, justice, and critical self-reflection. Rigor also entails heeding PEN's (2016) call for agency and racial justice as a part of progressive education and making good on Tom Little's (Little & Ellison, 2015) definition, which includes an "enduring commitment to social justice" (p. 52). This means going beyond a consciousness about diversity, justice, and access, and for TCS it means taking action.

TCS faculty and administration are deeply committed to naming and addressing issues of diversity and privilege, but acknowledge that knowing how to do so in effective and productive ways can be difficult. Some things that TCS has done to focus attention on these matters can be seen in part in the school's use of Teaching Tolerance's antibias framework, teacher professional development and curriculum work related to anti-oppressive education and White privilege, a revised school vision that highlights access and diversity, a strategic plan that calls for maintaining scholarship funds and financial aid at 10% of the school's operating budget, and a parent committee working on issues related to social justice, which includes developing an antibias toolkit of resources for other parents. But this work must be ongoing, and, admittedly, still more work needs to be done. These initiatives, while successful at moving the needle in limited ways, have not brought about extensive change. The school's teachers remain predominately White, female, and middle to upper middle class. There is also a struggle among teachers regarding their roles in bringing up topics of racial justice and privilege, even as the teachers have become more adept at handling sensitive topics in developmentally appropriate ways as they arise in the classroom. And while there has been progress in attracting students of color, there is significant room for improvement in this area.

Related to this consciousness is that progressive education does not claim that children's learning experiences should always be completely self-directed, fun, or easy. Rigor is related to the notion of challenge, and challenge is something progressive educators actively seek for each learner. When students are appropriately engaged in academic as well as social–emotional arenas, working at the cusp of their individual and collective comfort zones and pushed to see things differently or from multiple perspectives, they often achieve, learn, and create beyond perceived limits. Students, as well as teachers and administrators, should be supported in their attempts to innovate, adjust, and learn from missteps and mistakes as part of their own developmental journey. Students and teachers alike should be encouraged to have assumptions challenged and to challenge assumptions. At the same time, it has to be recognized that mistakes by teachers and administrators, in the choices they make, may have unintended consequences for students. And yet, many progressive schools see these potential missteps as much less severely detrimental than the standardized test-based, deficit measuring of teaching and the evaluation systems of more-prevalent teaching models.

Developmentally appropriate levels of challenge promote creative risk taking, help students to develop perseverance and tenacity, lead to a lasting feeling of accomplishment when obstacles are overcome, and empower students to be accountable for their own learning and work. Barriers, including failure and mistakes, are a necessary part of this process. Indeed, there must be moments of discomfort in every child's learning trajectory, and students achieve deep understanding by working through and toward an idea or skill that was initially difficult. Within this pursuit of an alternative approach, rigor is not reduced to mere facts or percentiles, but comes to the forefront in the classroom as an intellectual journey in and for powerful learning.

What is at stake here in fighting for this definition of rigor, and for this vision of progressive, democratic schools? Nothing less than our children's future. The rigid adherence to "standards"—however well-articulated or well-researched those standards may be—is harmful for children. The associated deficit model of learning fosters competition, threatens children's innate curiosity and intrinsic motivation to learn, and reduces the wide range of talents and gifts children possess to a very narrow focus on reading, writing, and arithmetic tasks. It deadens the imagination, the curiosity, and the power of children's voices and ideas. Progressive educators like those at TCS choose instead to embrace joy, wonder, and curiosity in teaching and learning. Through emergent curriculum and democratic processes, teachers and students can work alongside one another to model an innovative approach that transcends today's problematic educational landscape.

CHAPTER 3

Inverting the Curriculum, Finding Cracks, and Engaging Students

Brian D. Schultz, Jennifer McSurley, and Milli Salguero

During Jennifer's first year of teaching in an urban neighborhood school, she really wanted to teach to her conscience and explore ways to connect with her students. Jennifer self-identifies as a teacher who champions inquiry-based approaches. Deeply committed to justice in and out of the classroom, Jennifer sought ways to push aside the required curriculum for one that would allow both her and her students to be engaged and to do justice work. As a graduate student learning to be a teacher, Jennifer enrolled in my middle school curriculum and philosophy course. In this class, I utilized a social action curriculum project framework that relied on and was influenced by ideas and steps related to the Center for Civic Education's Project Citizen to demonstrate how curriculum could be democratic, justice-based, action-oriented, and integrate subject areas. Rather than simply teaching about this frame, Jennifer and her peers in the college classroom actually engaged in doing social action curriculum projects of their own.

TO TEACH INTO CURRICULAR CRACKS

A SACP framework is an approach to theorizing curriculum with students. Keenly local in nature, the method provides students and teachers in a specific classroom with the autonomy and authority to develop curriculum that is important, relevant, and responsive to their interests. A SACP is therefore a representation of problem-based learning and at its very heart is a means for teachers to engage their students in a Freirean (2000) problem-posing curriculum. Students identify an issue, problem, or theme that centers on a local or societal point of contention. Neither teachers nor outside agencies preconceive the issue. Instead, through classroom deliberation, students decide the problem. Students are forced to relate to the world around them in

32

working toward identifying and solving issues that concern them. Students contemplate possible alternative solutions by studying multiple sides to the issue. As the work progresses, the SACP scaffolds contingent action planning and techniques of participation as a means to work through and solve the problem. Through this process and the various modes of action planning, the SACP allows for learning critical skills related to democratic processes and encouraging political engagement. The SACP framework allows both the teacher and the students to challenge so-called educational reforms that focus on punitive or deficient orientations. And the SACP centers the consciousness of the students on their own questions as to what will be learned, why it will be learned, and how it will be learned. Students enact cooperative learning in order to enhance their immediate environments as they better their communities. In this model, students thus become readers of their world(s), working to solve issues relevant and meaningful to them (Freire, 2000).

In the classroom experiences of a SACP, the innate curiosities and challenges that young people face in their lives fuel continuous learning. The students' concerns and interests become foci of their decisionmaking and problem solving. The emergent curriculum becomes a guiding structure as the students pursue knowledge, information, and skills to complete tasks. When provided with a different sort of learning that actually revolves around them, students—especially children who have been taught in/through a top-down and noninquiry approach—are exposed to a framework of teaching and learning apart from the mainstream. In such spaces, competencies associated with democratic processes are learned, practiced, and experienced.

A SACP approach requires that students in classrooms immerse themselves in the practice of democratic engagement. Through full immersion, the teacher may connect content that emerges to state standards, if there are expectations from a school administrator, for example. Grappling with content-specific and transferable skills, students learn by doing as they navigate the effort to solve the problem. The SACP can be seen as a way to teach controversial issues in the classroom (Hess, 2009). Simultaneously, students learn firsthand and experientially how to participate in the direct action and mainstream practices related to participatory democracy. Students also learn when to utilize the public sphere to gain support and achieve results. This pedagogical method allows for political engagement and efficacy; students can become learners through participation rather than being taught through traditional ways. This is critical because most public schools purport to teach students citizenship, but actually do not provide students with participatory or change-oriented experiences. If schools really are to expect citizenship as a result of schooling experiences, they must find a way to inculcate it in students through such practices. Unfortunately, the approach carries a connotation that the teachers have an agenda (a political agenda) beyond simply giving their students the opportunity to engage politically, democratically, and collaboratively.

While schools tout productive citizenship in a democratic society as a key outcome of teaching and learning, current models produce citizen definitions that presume obedience, compliance, and rule-following. The SACP instead provides for engagement as seen in the possibilities of Westheimer and Kahne's (2004) pathbreaking work. Their research shows how the "good citizen" may take three different forms in classrooms: personally responsible, participatory, and justice-oriented. They observe that many teachers, unfortunately, focus on developing citizens who are only personally responsible (i.e., the promotion of charity, service, and character). Instead, they purport, teachers may nurture more nuanced participatory or even justice-oriented conceptualizations that center around instilling actions that challenge the status quo and are agency-focused. Following Westheimer and Kahne, we contend that there is little doubt as to why children, especially those in middle schools, adopt a disinterested attitude regarding citizenship. As the current culture of public schools focuses more and more on rigor associated with testing, how can we expect curricula to focus on such justice-related incarnations that revolve around social issues? With the restrictions on what to teach, challenges about meeting standards, and artificial timelines of learning that require teachers to keep pace with their colleagues, we contend that teachers must exploit cracks in the traditional curriculum, so that what occurs in the classroom is engaging, relevant, and meaningful.

At a time when the pressure placed on educators for student achievement is great, the SACP offers an opportunity for teachers to truly engage their students and provide them with opportunities to learn skills that will be meaningful in both academic matriculation and life. The learning by its very nature is robust but not rigid, has high expectations not based on testing, and emerges from questions that provoke and motivate students, especially since the nexus for the questions comes from the young people. Students can accumulate a wealth of experiences that provide them with an ongoing and developing sense of political and civic engagement, and teach them skills of negotiation, organizing, and navigating complex systems— abilities that undoubtedly will help them succeed in and out of school. Further, a SACP often pushes students into highly contested public spaces. In the public sphere, students are forced to seek knowledge in authentic environments where obstacles must be overcome in order to solve problems and make decisions. No longer acting as depositors of knowledge, teachers are emboldened to take on the role of facilitators in order to help guide the inquiries of their students.

NARRATIVE POINTS-OF-ENTRY

Through experiences from a college course in middle school curriculum and philosophy (in which Brian was the professor), Jennifer learned how to use SACPs. The course was designed to provide students a direct experience engaging in a SACP for themselves. Within the course context, college students engaged in SACPs that were of interest and relevant to them. Through her immersion experiences in the college course, Jennifer applied these experiences and transferred her learning to that of her own middle school classroom.

The SACP framework allows Jennifer to teach within the cracks in order to provide students critical pedagogical opportunities in her middle school classroom. In the next section, Jennifer presents narrative vignettes written about her middle school teaching experiences following engagement in SACPs with her students. The narrative emerges through storytelling of her teaching experiences in a midwestern, urban, diverse, medium-sized district school (approximately 43% White, 33% Black, 11% Latino, 9% Asian, 3% multiracial; 52% designated low income). Analysis of a teacher's "personal practical knowledge" (Clandinin & Connelly, 2000, p. 3) and elements of teacher lore as praxis—what William Schubert (1991) argues is the knowledge creation teachers engage in as they practice curriculum, theorize, and learn from their own experiences—provide opportunities to seek meaning and generate thick descriptions. Further, this form of narrative inquiry is reflective of and consistent with the critical, democratic pedagogy afforded to students in a SACP.

A multiplicity of data informed Jennifer's vignettes: classroom dialogue, informal interviews, student artifacts, and her reflective journaling. Jennifer's narrative is analyzed within classroom context and through subsequent reflection. The storytelling includes specific points-of-entry to Jennifer's interactions with students, colleagues, and administrators to portray her experience of feeling shackled to a mandated curriculum while finding opportunities to teach in critical ways. These points-of-entry were not predetermined. Rather, Jennifer chose to tell stories of her experience in her own way. Jennifer reveals parts of her experience and leaves out others—a hallmark of interpretive, critical inquiry. Importantly, if one of Jennifer's students, colleagues, or administrators were to tell such stories, they might be very different.

Mandates, Expectations, and Teaching in the Cracks

During the first week of school in my first year of teaching I met with the English language arts curriculum coordinator. The meeting was brief but to the point: He provided me with the curriculum that I was mandated to follow for the school year. As I contemplated the confinement, my new colleague reminded me how important following the guidelines would be, especially because of the district's quarterly testing.

The rigid, fast-paced, and traditional curriculum booklet made me wonder how I was going to find space to incorporate a social action curriculum project. I wanted to jump in right away to justice-oriented teaching, but I wanted to make a good impression and was fearful of rocking the boat.

Initially, I simply found it impossible to teach for social justice. I knew I was always held accountable for what my students learn, but the top-down expectations added intense pressure. Beyond the curriculum, I had to contend with quarterly testing, preparation for state achievement tests, and regular classroom observations from my principal, district administrators, and my first-year teaching mentor—all "looking out for me" but clearly keeping a careful eye toward implementing the curriculum. Added to this were daily meetings with my colleagues, weekly meetings with my principal, and monthly meetings with other faculty. These all seemingly took away my hopes of finding ways to develop curriculum that would provide for political engagement with the young people in front of me.

Although I felt initially defeated with all the pressure and meetings, I searched for cracks within the curriculum's framework so that I could fly under the radar with administrators. I needed to honor why I got into teaching in the first place and had to realize my goals of teaching in relevant and responsive ways. The opportunity I planned for was during creative writing, outlined in the 4th quarter. Surprisingly, creative writing was designed as process- and skill-based and was to "be taught" after the Quarterly Assessment. Would this be my chance to use methods, texts, and pedagogies I believed would work best with students?

To Be or Not to Be: Social Justice Teaching

In anticipation of the upcoming quarter in which I was going to take the leap, I met with a 10-year veteran teacher to discuss my ideas to engage students via SACPs. When I relayed my plans that I had been (im)patiently waiting to implement, my seemingly progressive colleague immediately squashed my ideas. "Jen, it's a wonderful idea," she exclaimed, "but I really don't think our kids will do much with these projects—we can barely get them to read a sentence without them complaining that it's too much work! How do you think they are going to act when you put this on their plates? Further, how are you going to make sure you follow the curriculum?" I saw my students' full potential and knew that part of their apathy centered around how the curriculum was organized;

it lacked student input. Although frustrated with her point of view since I knew my students might get motivated by this alternative approach, her comments also made me feel unsure of the entire idea, and I worried whether my students would be mature enough to take on serious issues beyond the classroom.

Despite what appeared to be obstructionist feedback from my colleague, I couldn't help but recall a professor's advice: "If you don't jump into teaching for social justice in your first year, you probably never will." Unfortunately, with the end of the year approaching, I really saw his point—I had been confined to the curriculum and to testing. I needed to shift the power dynamic from outside mandates to my local classroom.

"We Cannot Change Anything!" or "Getting to the Bottom of It"

Day 1 of SACPs, I nervously asked my class: "Do you think you have the power to make changes in the world today?" Darion responded, "You mean now or like when we're older?" Turning to Darion, Jeremy flatly stated, "We're just kids, we're never taken seriously, and we cannot change anything!"

In an instant the class was in an uproar! Darion, a charismatic boy who consistently exercised leadership skills, looked at Jeremy and loudly responded: "You just don't know what powers you have or how to use them!"

I asked everyone to relax as I continued: "Why is it important for you to be active in your learning? To know how to problem solve?"

My guiding questions prompted participation from virtually every student. As we discussed what we wanted to change, large lists developed. I wondered how classes would limit activities to a few core issues, but as topics were discussed students began debating the issues and narrowing down the topics. Surprisingly, my worry about tailoring lists subsided as the students self-selected topics based on personal interests.

While we were delving deep into a discussion of community problems during 3rd hour, my department chair walked into the classroom unannounced to observe me. She had no idea what was going on. I thought to myself: "This is it! You are going to be fired because she won't know what the heck you are doing. How will I explain this? Back yourself up, Jen! You knew this was coming!" When I snapped back into reality, I went with my lesson plan; what else could I do? (See Figures 3.1–3.4).

The class was already in self-chosen groups, deliberating about the issues they had identified. Both my chair and I were drawn to one particular group. The students were in a heated discussion, deliberating about whether the issue should be "world hunger" or "hunger in the city." As I challenged the group with questions that would narrow down the topic, the group decided to focus on making local changes in the city to, as they articulated, "put a dent in the problem."

Figure 3.1. Jennifer's lesson plans introducing social action curriculum projects to her students. (Photo: Jennifer McSurley)

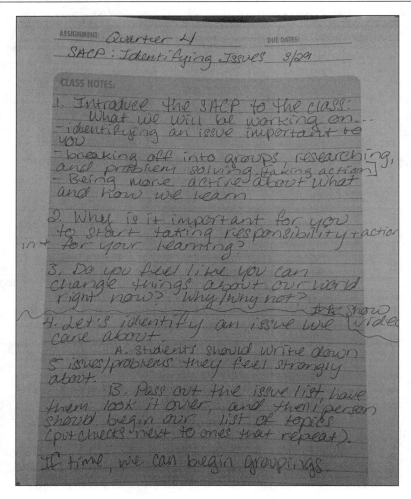

The department chair appeared interested, but remained silent while taking notes. When the bell rang, she asked, "How is what they are doing aligned with the curriculum?" I was prepared for such questions, but answering them wasn't easy. I knew I was going against the grain. Cautiously, I explained how I had interpreted the creative writing curriculum for 4th quarter. I expressed how these projects had the potential to cover so much more through writing: problem solving, critical thinking, and interactive learning—let alone the political engagement and real-world problem solving that I sought. As the next class entered the room, she left without comment. Later, she and I exchanged

Figure 3.2. Jennifer's lesson plan to help students identify topics and issues in the community. (Photo: Jennifer McSurley)

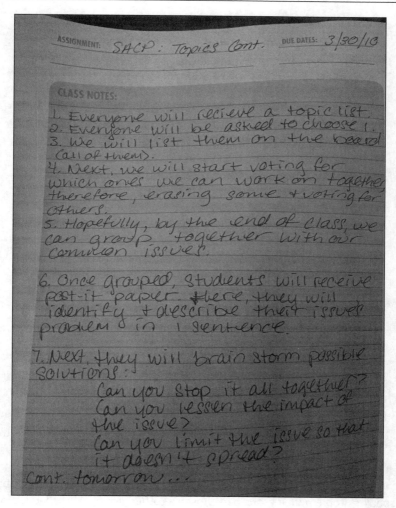

emails; she was definitely concerned and as she put it, "determined to get to the bottom of it."

Struggles and Opportunities

Students began to work in their groups, identifying their problem/issue and writing about it, creating a solution, and researching. While many groups were working extremely hard—harder than I had seen them engage all year—there were some groups that appeared to be putting forth minimal effort. I began

Figure 3.3. Jennifer's lesson plans focused on solutions and research related to topics chosen by students. (Photo: Jennifer McSurley)

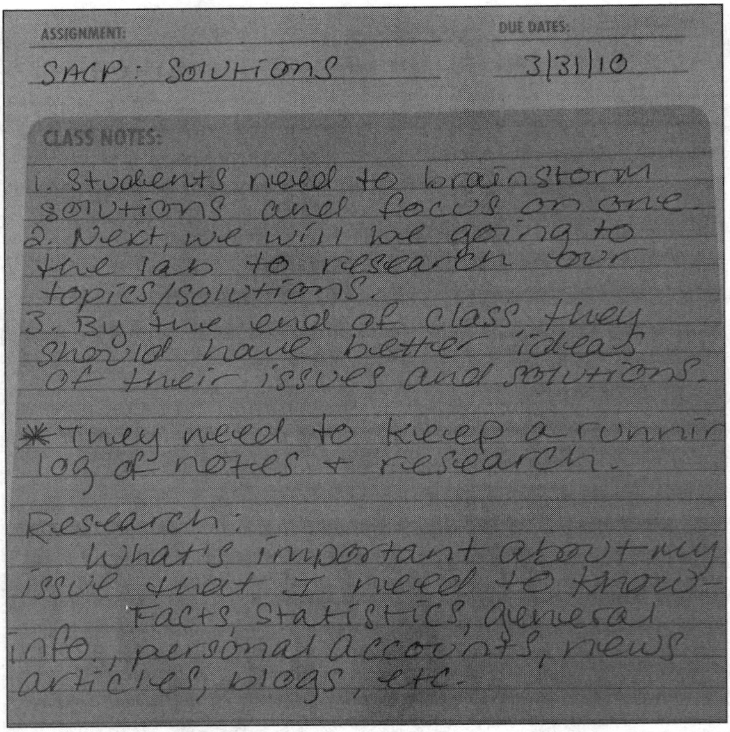

to wonder whether my colleague's apprehension and my department chair's skepticism were warranted. In my journal, all I could do was ask questions: Do the students not have the right group chemistry? Do they not care about their issue enough? Did I misstep along the way?

In retrospect, and although I cannot be certain, what seemed problematic for these groups centered on the fact that they were not as passionate about the specific problem their group had chosen as other groups. My reflective journal highlighted my pondering about some students' difficult home lives and the trickiness of pushing them to think about problems they faced outside of school as the projects threatened the defense mechanisms they had built around the turmoil in their home lives. I hoped that if I was able to coach them with persistence, the SACP could be an opening for them to change their attitudes about this project in particular, and also about school more generally. (See Figure 3.4 for an excerpt of Jennifer's journal.)

In contrast to a couple of low-energy groups, an all-male group self-titled Teen Talk was already digging deep into provocative issues. Led by Darion, the

Figure 3.4. Excerpt from Jennifer's teacher reflective journal. (Photo: Jennifer McSurley)

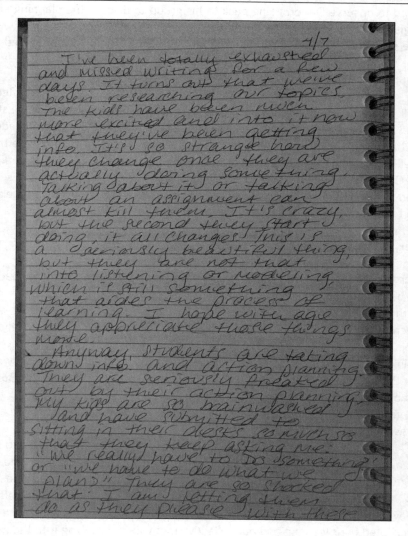

group was discussing questions that are not usually entertained in a classroom, pertaining to sex, drugs, violence, relationships, and peer pressure. Getting ahead of themselves, they were already thinking through a solution to the fact that important topics about their lives were never discussed in school. Their idea was to run an 8th-grade teen summit in which they would select a diverse group of students to have discussions with the school community. Immediately, Darion wanted to take the plan to the principal. I told him that they needed to research the topics and formulate a proposal first. I was worried that my pushback would deter Darion's fervor, but I was heartened to observe Darion going back to his group to discuss the planning and logistics of a summit. After further detail gathering, Darion and I met with the principal after school; Darion did all the talking. The principal agreed to the summit, with some ground rules of course, but expressed how she was impressed with the group and his work!

The principal may have been impressed, and although groups such as Teen Talk were in full gear and their projects were taking on lives of their own, I still had the 4th-quarter creative writing expectations hovering over me. I needed to tie creative writing into the SACP. It was highly important to articulate this well or else I knew that I would, at the very least, lose all credibility regarding SACPs. I was feeling the pressure. My goal was to leverage similar processes I had taught previously for some new writing that would be nonfiction and related to the SACP.

Sex, Drugs, and Teen Talk

The Teen Talk group members were so eager to take advantage of the spaces to develop their own curriculum. Several members approached me, asking me if they could cover topics like drugs and sex in their summit. Whereas I was secretly apprehensive because of potential administrative and parental fallout about teaching taboo topics, I tried not to show it to the students. "What do you think you need to do if you plan on discussing these topics and having answers for them?" I queried, and without hesitation Darion retorted, "Research!" Guided by the freedom to inquire and write about topics that fascinated them, the group researched subtopics while collaborating to create a full discussion and presentation for the summit.

Although they were excited about the prospects of the schoolwide attention, the group struggled to conceptualize something that would be as meaningful to others as it was for them. They constantly wanted to check in with me to make sure their progress was on the right track. They questioned whether they "were doing it right," but at the same time their questions and concerns facilitated their learning and our collective motivation for taking it to the next level for the summit. Moreover, the learning processes that I had tried to communicate to the chair and other colleagues were exactly how I saw students engaging. What was fascinating was that I did not have all the answers, and in many check-ins with students they were pushing me to learn topics in ways that I had not imagined prior to working with them.

This sort of zeal stayed consistent throughout their efforts and was apparent after the students worked hard at making their school summit a reality. Because topics were selected by students schoolwide, the panel was well attended.

The group even wanted to continue after the end-of-day bell rang to go home! It was clear to all in attendance that Darion was proud of himself and his group.

Because this group did not want the SACP efforts to end with the school day, they decided to take the discussion out of school. The group formed a youth engagement venue at the local YMCA to host similar events and dialogues. Darion confided in me: "Mrs. McSurley, being a former 'troubled teen,' I know what it's like to have questions about all of these crazy issues that we kids deal with. I know that when I didn't get the right answers, it led me down some bad paths. This is why I've decided to continue these summits at the 'Y.'" Darion and his peers stressed that they were interested in educating others in order to help teens make better life choices.

Hunger and Community Activism

The hopefulness associated with Teen Talk is also evident in another SACP. This group, For a Change, focused on hunger and feeding people in our city. After researching the topic, they centered their action planning on issues that, at first glance, seemed more focused on superficial charity than justice orientations. They wanted to make sure the community was aware of the hungry's plight and wanted to find ways to provide for people. As their project went deeper, not only did students hold a food drive and connect with a food bank, but they also pushed for awareness through a poster and video campaign that went beyond notions of "giving" and charity.

When I questioned them about what appeared to be the often-simplistic idea of charity, the group dug deep in discussions about how they could effect lasting community change. Their discussions were nuanced because they found the issue to be more complex than they initially thought. Fighting hunger for some members was a social responsibility, but for others bigger questions about why people went hungry and society's role were imperative to why they wanted to be involved. The issue of charity versus equity and justice is complex, particularly for middle schoolers. When the students were challenged and prompted, together we wrestled with the nuances of a continuum related to this complicated issue. This, in turn, guided how we could participate in resolving the issue.

Several group members' comments struck a chord with me. Adeeva queried, "We only have food drives during Christmas. Why not any other times? What is wrong in our society that people can be needing food?" Keisha agreed, and perhaps saw an even bigger issue than her classmate was raising, when she retorted, "But, people really need food during those times and people are more likely to give during the holidays. How can we get people to give when it's not that time of year and get them to understand the bigger issue?"

Their questions furthered discussion. Another member raised the following notion: "We need facts about hunger and how many people are starving in our own neighborhoods. This will convince people because it has emotional appeal." Adeeva replied, "The challenge we really have is changing people's minds about giving anything. People need food all year long." Keisha stated, "Yeah, it's like understanding that if you have food for yourself and maybe some extra you can make a change. Imagine if we all felt like that!" As I listened, I observed their plan shifting from food-drive mode to changing people's minds about the idea of hunger.

Despite the dilemma the group confronted in private among themselves, their multiple avenues of action had food pouring into the classroom. Further, their documentary video about hunger was being played in all of my classes. After a month, For a Change asked me to help them deliver the food to the food bank. We showed up unannounced—perhaps a result of middle schoolers not thinking through all the parts of the process. Impressed by the students' enthusiasm and the amount of food in tow, the head of the food bank stopped his work to provide a tour and solicit students for volunteer opportunities, especially in areas beyond simply collecting food.

On the car ride back to school, Adeeva confided to me: "This experience has changed me in a way I cannot really describe. It feels good to work for my community." I challenged her with questions, since her statement sounded focused on charity again. Her classmate interjected, "It's been life-changing, and I want to keep doing more. I never used to think about issues like this in the world." Adeeva agreed, adding, "It's like I am thinking about things I didn't know mattered. Now, I can't stop thinking about these things."

Similar to the other group that wanted to continue, this group also approached me after the formal SACP ended. Alongside her groupmates, Keisha asked, "Did you hear about the food bank we donated to? It was on the news." Unaware of the grave issue, I let her continue. "We just heard that they are completely out of food, losing money, and in danger of shutting down!" In a follow-up meeting with me after school, the girls decided that they needed to go back to the research and organizing skills they had learned in class through the SACP.

Before I knew it, the school was involved in a comprehensive attempt to strengthen the food bank through efforts from the girls and others. The group produced posters that highlighted their newfound justice orientation. They told me they wanted my help in having a donation drive for the food bank. The girls were going to set up moneyboxes in each teacher's classroom as well as make posters and announcements. The food bank's dire situation had shocked them into action and urgency, and now they had tools to get the job done.

DEVELOPING SPACES TO ENGAGE

Introducing middle school students to the SACP process is fundamental to inspiring and motivating them within a traditional schooling framework. In Jennifer's classroom, the students engaged in SACPs through discussion and debate; the classroom became a space where students had liberty to deliberate on issues of importance to their lives. Through deliberation students felt compelled to engage in groupwork with others who shared similar interests. The SACPs related to talking about issues that mattered to the students and feeding people in the city, which helped the groups to share and envision what they ultimately were trying to accomplish. While adhering to the SACP framework, Jennifer and her students were able to develop a kind of classroom curriculum that was most responsive to their needs and interests.

Jennifer's narrative details the efforts of two groups as they used the challenge of the SACP to identify their issue, create a solution, research, and engage in action. (For teachers interested in a related model and curriculum materials that focus on public policy change, see the Center for Civic Education's Project Citizen at civiced.org/programs/project-citizen.) This is what "teaching in the cracks" is all about. The SACP was a gateway to raise an issue at hand in order to arrive at a shared goal. Jennifer was able to immerse her students in a SACP by exploiting openings in the state-outlined curriculum, which she nonetheless was following.

A traditional school classroom may be confined to a strict curriculum, which ultimately limits opportunities for active engagement. Contrary to traditional classroom structures, the core of a SACP effort offers a space to challenge social issues within school, thus promoting motivation and commitment. This space becomes vital for a SACP because active problem solving cannot be conducted theoretically. Jennifer's narrative offers insight into a traditional classroom working in a nontraditional manner. An issue relevant to the students' lives is discussed, followed by direct, problem-solving activity within the community and expectations of high achievement. The students' experiences represent the potential of what teaching and learning can accomplish outside of the confines of prescriptive instruction.

EMBRACING, NEGOTIATING, AND REVISITING CHALLENGES

Part of the process for students involved in a SACP is to grapple with the notion that they can make a difference in their lives in and outside of their classroom. Challenges and barriers will result. Although traditional school settings adhere to strict curricula in order to avoid divergence, a SACP develops opportunities to demonstrate that rich learning experiences can occur outside of a conventional framework. Importantly, outcomes are neither preconceived nor predetermined by the teacher or students. Instead, the varied processes of working to solve identified issues allow for learning to flourish organically. In Jennifer's narrative, we see how developing curricula with students is complex, thorough, and participatory. We also see how the processes of inquiry fueled discovery and learning. Importantly, this was not known at the onset but instead was discovered in the moments of critical engagement. Further, the vignettes show how the groups equally valued the process and worked toward an end goal, albeit to varying degrees.

Building understanding within the groups was a sticking point, although for reasons that differed depending on the students. This was most obvious when a group member was clearly disengaged from the group, not caring about the topic or taking action. This disinterest was a cause for reflection on Jennifer's part; it inevitably made her question her teaching methods and whether this approach to designing and developing curricula was able to reach all of her students. When students reach a point of disinterest, it can slow down the progress and formation of a well-defined action plan. This is important as it highlights the complex nature of engaging students in SACPs. This also takes place in groups that are heavily involved in their projects. Consider the critical moment when Jennifer prompts students to make sure they are thinking through issues related to awareness and justice, not simply focused on charity work.

The evolving process of SACPs requires that students refine the action plan as needed. This refining process is ongoing throughout the entire project and is a key part of the equation in facilitating transferable skills that students may take away from the experience. The students often face obstacles while involved in action planning, and this leads them to explore new directions to achieve their goals. Students are encouraged to continuously evaluate and reconsider the efficacy of their efforts. Such experiences echo the realities of our lives outside of the schoolhouse. Neither the teacher nor students are able to foresee how their actions will be received or the challenges they may face as they take on these issues.

A SACP is meant to push the totality of the curriculum, especially in middle school, although large questions remain. Can teaching curriculum "through the cracks" embrace the depths of all the knowledge that students should acquire? How will students learn all they are "supposed to know" according to state boards of education or textbook companies, while still gaining useful life skills? Perhaps the thought from a member of For a Change demonstrates the potential to transform how we think about classrooms. As Adeeva said earlier, her engagement in a SACP was a profound experience that was life-changing in ways she could not describe easily. Realizing that she previously had not thought about justice issues in the world, Adeeva commented that with this one powerful school experience, she wanted ways to "keep doing more."

As current and future teachers ponder curricular possibilities involved in a SACP, vast opportunities for pedagogical exploration occur. It is possible for traditional subject-area competencies, including effective persuasive writing, mathematical computations, oral presentations, and scientific reasoning, to be transformed into integrated teaching areas fully capable of encompassing politically engaged social action. Motivating students to focus on relevant issues associated with a SACP becomes less challenging than making sure those same students adhere to the strict confines of a traditional classroom. Power lies herein: Young people choose topics important to them and then are provided with spaces and opportunities, and ultimately challenged with responsibilities, to solve the problem they selected, while meeting the expectations set within a mandated curriculum.

What are the outcomes of a SACP within an era of high-stakes hyper-accountability? This is an essential question to reflect on in the current climate of outcomes-oriented standardization. The initial purpose of a SACP is clearly to address problems identified by students in classrooms while honoring their interests. SACPs provide opportunities, often absent from classrooms today, to practice democratic dialogue. Beyond the surface, however, SACPs are not necessarily restricted to such objectives. SACPs are also tools for educators who want to teach in engaging yet possibly subversive ways while still adhering to the outside mandates. Further, outcomes related to the SACP may not be known prior to engagement but instead emerge through participation. Teachers' and students' action-planning processes have the deep potential to push against the status quo and develop significant skill sets in the process. In so doing, the SACP provides teachers an ability to teach under the radar of curricular expectations if and as necessary, while developing young people's competencies for participating and navigating within a democracy.

CHAPTER 4

The Localizing Ebola Project
A Student-Led Emergent Curriculum

An Interview with Teacher Will Hudson

In a compelling example of the emergent nature of a social action curriculum project, students in Will Hudson's classroom at The Children's School initially became curious about the broad topic of sickness and death. They soon immersed themselves in study about the global Ebola virus epidemic as a topical starting point. As students researched this topic, they began a journey with their teacher, becoming formidable middle-level experts on the resources and demographics of countries in West Africa. I began referring to the students' multiple month effort as the Localizing Ebola Project since their inquiry into Ebola in Africa led them back home again to look more deeply at local health issues. As they questioned everything from access to medicine and education globally, they began to examine local sanitation practices in their school. Wondering whether they could effect changes to promote health and wellness on a local level, they identified different methods for analysis, action, and engagement. They surveyed the school community, cultured bacteria, studied chemistry, produced soap from raw materials, and developed an awareness campaign to not only highlight their learning but also seek ways to change behaviors and practices among those in the school community.

The interview that follows sheds light on how one teacher supported his students in the curriculum that emerged from their interests as they originated and developed their project. The interview was generated from several questions that were constructed in advance to elicit key information. Others grew out of the conversation as it proceeded.

CHOOSING A TOPIC

Brian Schultz: I understand that your students came up with a lot of different topics that they were excited to study for the year. In particular, though, the first project that they wanted to take on had to do with the topic of sickness and death. How did the students arrive at this topic?

Will Hudson: Basically, we went through the process of them identifying questions and concerns that they had about themselves and the world, and then went through the process of having them generate themes around their questions. Over the period of about a week or so, I had them putting together questions at home and at school, and then sharing them. Then we wrote them all out on pieces of paper, cut them out, and then they sorted them by topics that they identified. After that they named them. Sickness and death was one of the names that they gave to a group of questions that they had generated.

There were others. Environmental problems, I think, were one. The future. Stuff like that. And the sickness and death—and then we voted. We figured out which one we wanted to touch on first, and that's what they chose.

Brian Schultz: As a teacher, total macabre topic, right? Sickness and death. The irony is that it's so perfect for early adolescents. That makes sense. They're wondering who they are in this world and what's going on in this world. Sickness and death seems like an appropriate topic of interest, but in the school? In a classroom?

Will Hudson: One of the things that really pushed us in that direction was the idea of after-death—near-death experiences and their fascination with that. What does that mean? What is that? Recognizing that there was a scientific explanation to it and also a spiritual explanation to it, but still being fascinated and, I think, them wrestling with this idea of existence and nonexistence. It was just twisting their brains a little bit and that led us into it.

Then when they said that's where they wanted to go, it was really like, "Okay, this is great. Mr. Hudson's going to be known for—" Last year it was discrimination for months on end. This year it's sickness and death. It's just these heavy topics. I don't know if I was unnerved by it, though.

Brian Schultz: Did you try to reframe it at all?

Will Hudson: Not really. When they identified it, I wanted to make sure —to reiterate, like, "Okay, this is what you guys want to call it? This is where you want to go?" They were definite about that.

The only reframing I did was saying, "Okay, if we're going to talk about sickness and death, then we also need to talk about health and wellness." Just as a counterpoint that it seemed to me was a necessary component of that, that if we're going to talk about what it means to be sick—and the students actually asked this, too. They'd asked the question. "Well, is not being sick the same thing as being well? Is that the same thing as health?" They were splitting these hairs really early on.

Brian Schultz: How do you get at the issue, though, of something that is topically generated? The topic is sickness and death, but how did you turn it into a problem to solve and maybe answer the question of how the project might be characterized as evolving over time?

Will Hudson: Right. I think for them it was tough at the beginning. I told them this is great, but there has to be what I was calling an action step. There has to be some component of this project where we do something, where we identify something and we move on that and try to effect some sort of positive change within our community. That was tough for them. I think that they saw sickness and death as the problem. I think also one of the comments that was made was, "It's hard for us to make a decision about what we should do or what problems we want to try to solve before we—we need to learn more about the topic."

CONNECTING TO CURRENT EVENTS

Brian Schultz: Okay. Then that's where they started studying the Ebola epidemic?

Will Hudson: Right. That was hot at the time. That was all in the news. It was one of those coincidences that it was there. It appeared in front of us. That's where we started to focus. Then my role, I felt at that time, was to try to unpack and reveal the things that I wanted them to focus on a little bit. It was trying to steer the project in a direction I thought it should go without me overtly saying, "Hey, this is what it has to be." The Ebola stuff was in the news a lot. There was interest in that. We were talking about that. We started off by talking about health disparities and just looking at the statistics, looking at how many cases of sickness were being recorded in a specific country, and also what was the mortality rate in that specific country. Comparing those two numbers, and then also looking at education rates among boys and girls and then looking at those numbers and seeing—they were trying to find correlations between, perhaps, education and rate of disease. Looking at the economic situation in these different countries and trying to find correlations. Trying to find some sort of connections there.

The one part that I did drive is that, as we were working through this, we saw some correlations. We were able to start identifying, like, "Wow, there appears to be a connection here between health and economics and health and education." This idea of access. Basically, if you're poor, you don't have as much access to healthcare. If you're poor, you also don't have as much access to education, which affects quality of life as well. I think when they started seeing those connections was when we started to flesh out this idea of maybe where we could act.

Brian Schultz: Your students became formidable 6th-grade experts—middle-level experts—in the economics, the education, the access to healthcare of several West African countries that were being affected by the Ebola epidemic.

Will Hudson: Yes. I think so. One of the things that we decided was that—and I felt that it was important—if we're going to spend this much time studying about just this disease that's taking place and these ideas that are in the news, we had to, almost out of respect, take some time and actually learn about the countries themselves and the culture of the countries and their historical backgrounds.

I think we took about 2 weeks where the kids worked with partners. Each group studied one of the countries that were being affected. They spent 2 weeks researching and creating presentations. We generated what we wanted to have represented within the presentations. There were things that I wanted and then things that they brought in as well. Over that period of time, I feel like they really learned a lot and really engaged with the culture as well as what was taking place there.

SHIFTING LOCAL AND TAKING ACTION

Brian Schultz: From that point of studying countries in Africa and learning about the culture and interrogating those spaces, how, then, did they make the turn to the local community? I'm really fascinated with the idea of this overarching hot-button issue in the news then translating to wanting to take action among the school community.

Will Hudson: It developed as we went along, going back to this idea of access to education and economics as being these two really critical components

in terms of factors that affect health and being able to home in on that.
I think for them, they were at a point where they were pretty quick to
pick up on, "Well, if you have more money, then that's going to give you
more access to healthcare. If you have more education, that's going to
give you more access to, well, more money, or having more education
will allow you to know more about how to engage in practices that will
help keep you healthy." That's one of the things that we saw in some of
those countries, that there was just a lack of education. Then there were
also cultural practices as well that were affecting incidence and transmis-
sion rates of disease.

Then trying to bring that home a little bit, what I think was really interesting is that often there is this idea of engaging with the community.
They're 6th-graders. Their worlds are expanding. Their sense of place
is widening, but their community is still this school. Oak Park and the
places where they live, that's their community, but they're not as deeply
engaged with that either.

It's just this really idyllic type [of community that many of them live
in]—we had this conversation as well. We were talking about Maslow's
hierarchy of needs and talking about having those needs met. Then you
ask them, "Well, how do you feel when you walk out of your house and
you go take a walk around your neighborhood?" It's like, "Oh, I feel
really great. It's really peaceful. It's really nice. I love to go out. There
are parks. It's beautiful." Then I was like, "Okay, well, right down the
street from where I live, a guy was shot on the corner. How do you
think people in that neighborhood feel about walking around their
neighborhood? Do you think there's a difference there?"

Brian Schultz: This question is quite a challenge for 6th-graders because you
are pushing them to see beyond their own experiences. Whereas I can
see how this connects with the class' study of West Africa, I am curious
how this and other discussions about community brought the sickness
and death project into the school setting for the students to take contingent action.

Will Hudson: I think they really see the school community as their community. That's where it went—talking about access, talking about money
and education, and then also brainstorming things that were taking place
in our school. One of the things that came up is when Miss Martin says,
"Hey, everybody, be sure you wash your hands. Are you washing your
hands regularly? It's cold and flu season." They questioned whether or
not kids in the school were actually washing their hands.

Figure 4.1. Student-made bacteria cultures. (Photo: Brian Schultz)

We also had a conversation that I remember where we were saying, "Okay, well, if this is the community, if we're talking about engaging with our school community and we've identified either money or education, where can we effect change?" Being that this is a private school with tuition, we were thinking, "Well, if we're all here together, then money's not really an issue, but where can we do something?" They realized, "Well, we can do something to educate the rest of the community."

Brian Schultz: Is this where, then, they started their action steps, the contingent action planning around doing something about that issue? What was it that they did?

Will Hudson: The wheels started turning at that point. Handwashing became the thing on which we focused. One of the things that we wanted to do was some sort of experiment to determine whether or not handwashing even makes a difference.

We came up with the idea of doing bacteria cultures and culturing our hands and creating an experiment, or an investigation, to try to determine whether or not that had an effect (see Figure 4.1). Going through that process. Then, I think, we also determined we needed to make some sort of a survey. These were just constant conversations that were going on in the class. We're sitting down and just hashing it out, trying to figure out what our next steps were together.

Brian Schultz: You weren't saying, "Today, class, we're going to do a survey."

Will Hudson: No.

Brian Schultz: "Today, class, we're going to swab our hands and culture the bacteria."

Will Hudson: No. I think many times I'd have it in the back of my head, and they would get really frustrated with me. They're savvy, so pretty quickly they latch onto the idea that quite often I do have the answer that I want them to give me, but I'm not going to tell them what it is. In the back of my head, I'm thinking, "Yeah, bacteria cultures would really be great."

Or a survey. If we want to find out about what people are thinking, then the surveys are a means to learning that—but they had never done a survey before. They had never even really completed a survey before. It's not something that was really within their realm of experience. It was this process of trying to throw out little kernels of ideas to get them to latch onto it. "Well, how would we go about doing that? If we wanted to know if people do wash their hands regularly, how would we do that? What other types of questions would we want to try to answer? Is it just about do they wash their hands after they go to the bathroom? Is it other times of the day?" Then having them stumble across it. "Oh, well, we could do a survey." "Oh, yeah, absolutely you could do a survey. You figured it out. Great."

I had an idea in my head, like, "Well, this would be a great opportunity to do this thing." Then trying to get them—working through it concurrently. I think that's the thing, that in my mind, it's always so critical that they own it, that it's theirs. I'm really, especially at this point in the year, careful about trying to make sure that whatever we did decide to do, they felt like it was theirs. Maybe if it wasn't 100% their idea, at least it was something that they bought into and they owned. It wasn't me.

Brian Schultz: Can you tease this idea of them owning their idea? Maybe in the broader scheme of how your previous experiences played out in teaching.

Will Hudson: For the experiment, we were going to do these bacteria cultures and the handwashing stuff. Well, one way that we could have done it is I could have devised the entire experiment and then said, "Okay, here you go. You follow the directions." You walk them through it, which in my mind is not—that's not an experiment at that point. That's them demonstrating whether or not they can follow directions and doing what I'm telling them to do.

Where on the other hand, it was, "Okay, we're going to do this handwashing experiment. We're going to see whether or not it makes a difference. Okay. You now have to devise the experiment. What is this going to look like? What is it that you're trying—what is the question that you're trying to ask? What is your hypothesis? What are going to be—what are your procedures?"

Brian Schultz: Okay, so take us to that. They're doing the handwashing. They're culturing bacteria right now. What are they doing? How are they doing that? Are they rubbing one another's hands with cotton swabs?

Will Hudson: Well, that was part of the conversation. I got the materials for them, and then I basically said, "Here's what we have. Figure out how to make it work." There were all these different types of things, like the agar. That was new to us. They had to prepare the agar and to put it into the Petri dishes. I basically gave them the instructions that came with the kit and said, "This is how you do it." That's what they did. They set that whole thing up.

With the cotton swabs, with the swabbing of the hands, we realized that to do that, we had to be consistent about how we were going to do that every time. That's where I came in. I asked, "Okay, well, how are you going to swab the hands? Are you just going to—are you going to swab just the palm? Are you going to swab the fingers?" Even down to, "Are you going to swab from the tip of the finger down to the palm, or are you going to swab from the palm out to the tip of the finger?" Whatever it is, you have to make that decision and then you have to be consistent with that.

Brian Schultz: When they did it, did they actually follow the guidelines?

Will Hudson: Absolutely. Absolutely they did. They were very specific about that. What happened, though, in the end was that there were other variables that we didn't control for. They had their procedures, they had written them all up, and they followed them to a T. From start to finish, they set everything up and carried the experiment out on their own.

One thing that we didn't think of was that they were trying so hard to keep their materials sterile that every time they were moving anything or doing anything, they were hand sanitizing. They were doing all this hand sanitizing, but then the people who were sanitizing their hands were also the ones that were going to have their hands swabbed. All of a sudden, it's like—and I'm thinking about this at the time, watching it, going like, "Oh, okay, we maybe didn't consider this part."

Then for whatever reason, at some point they were like, "Okay, we should swab the totally filthy way," where you go into the bathroom, maybe go through the motions of using the restroom, but you don't wash your hands. You don't do anything. Then do it another way, where you just put water on your hands. Then actually wash your hands and test each time. They went through it, but at the end, when we started getting our cultures—our cultures started growing—that's when we realized, "Okay, there's stuff here that we didn't plan for."

Brian Schultz: Take us to when the kids are realizing, "Oh, wait, maybe we didn't control for all the variables." What was the conversation?

Will Hudson: Things started growing. We pulled them out and were looking at them, and we were like, "Huh. There doesn't really appear to be a whole lot of difference between—" There's no consistency, I think is what it was.

Brian Schultz: What did the kids do about it?

Will Hudson: At that point, we figured, "Okay, well, we need to go back. We need to think about it again." They were aware that we had to control for variables, but then they did it and then it became a conversation of "Okay, what variables did we not account for?" What was really great about that is that if I had created this experiment for them, if I had come up with it from scratch, would I have accounted for those variables? I don't know. Maybe. Maybe not.

During that discussion, since it was theirs, it was like, "Okay, we made this thing. For all practical purposes, we followed the method." They wrote it all out. It looked great, but they were realizing, "Wow, we made this thing, and our results are inconclusive." Instead of seeing that as a failure, as in, "Oh, well, we messed this up," it was like, "Well, actually, no, you didn't really mess up anything. You just ran the experiment, and now you're reflecting on that experiment and recognizing that there's some components of this that we didn't account for." Then the discussion became, "Well, that's the science. That's the learning." They realized it. Then the question was, "Okay, well, we recognize this. What do we do? What are the variables that we now have to account for?"

Brian Schultz: They were willing to do the—

Will Hudson: Absolutely. To do the whole thing—to set up all over again. For example, we had different people swabbing the Petri dish. Some people swabbed really hard, so it would tear up the agar and stuff like that. So the students were asking, "Okay, well, should we have three different people that swab the dishes, or should it just be one person and that's what their job is?" That's what it was. Together they were saying, "Okay, yeah. We need to have just one person who does the swabs."

They broke everything down so that everyone had a specific job and there wasn't all this overlap, which had caused some of the problems the first round.

Could we have done that the first time? I don't know. The thing is, all the kids wanted to get their hands swabbed. There's that thing. Everybody wanted their hand swabbed, and everybody wanted to be the swabber. They had to go through the process to realize that, well, maybe that's not the best way. So yeah. They redid it. We rewrote it, simplified it to some degree. We were able to fine-tune, and ask, "Okay, what is it that we're actually trying to measure here?" There were discussions around that as well.

Brian Schultz: You have two big projects going on at the same time in the sense that there's a survey being contemplated and developed, and then there's the culturing of bacteria that's happening. This is all under the bigger umbrella of wanting to make some impact or change on the local community and the sanitation practices of kids in the school.

Will Hudson: Right.

Brian Schultz: What else did they do in terms of taking action in other ways? What were some of the other experiences they had once they had survey data to make sense of and to analyze, once they started seeing what would happen with their bacteria cultures?

Will Hudson: Well, we got the survey. That process in itself probably took hours, the discussions that went around that. Putting together the data.

Brian Schultz: Well, I'm curious. The survey wasn't the end result, right? This survey was informational. What'd they find out on the survey?

Will Hudson: They started with the whole bathroom thing. That was the focus. Then one of the questions that they had on the survey was whether or not people washed their hands after coughing or blowing their nose, and they found that a really large, big percentage of students did not. So then, they were like, "Oh, okay. Here's something. Here's something. This we could actually, really focus on. The hand-washing thing as well, in the bathroom and stuff, but there's also this other component."

Then it became a matter of, well, they wanted to put together the campaign. They were thinking, "Oh, well, we have the data. We've done the science. We've done the research. We have our survey. We have the survey results." Then the survey was great because, again, it gave them that opportunity to pinpoint places, like, "We should focus on this. This is a place that we can focus on."

DEVELOPING AWARENESS AND ENGAGING OTHERS

Brian Schultz: This awareness campaign. What were the prongs of the awareness campaign?

Will Hudson: The awareness campaign. What did they do? One of the things we decided is that we should make soap. Then they wanted to distribute soap to every member of the school community. That was part of it. We did just a really basic glycerin soap, where they weighed it out and melted it down and added their fragrance and their colors and made 110 eight-ounce bars of soap that were individually wrapped and handed out to every student in the entire school. They created posters and drafted slogans.

We divvied up tasks a little bit, like who was more interested in what. One of the students came up with a variety of different slogans that they then worked together on to make posters, the posters that would go up all over the school. They wanted to have videos, so one student wrote a number of different handwashing, scenario-type, situational videos that they filmed and edited. There was a website that they created. That was a place—they called that their campaign headquarters. That was a place for them to have—they posted their videos there. They posted their survey data there. They had a fact a day that they posted there. They developed a mission statement that went there. There were those components.

Then throughout the school—they prepared everything, and then we went on break. The idea was to have everything ready so that after we got back from break we could start day one. They determined that the campaign should go on for 3 weeks because it takes 21 days, is what somebody came up with, to help create a habit.

They had a kickoff at one of the gatherings. First thing in the morning, they shared a fact a day with the entire school. They showed videos in the mornings. Then they also—geez, what else did they do? They learned about soap chemistry and the molecular structure of soap and how soap works so that when they distributed soap, they created a poster to demonstrate this and went from classroom to classroom and gave a talk to each classroom, explaining to them how soap worked and how it helped to remove bacteria and other pathogens from your hands, and then distributed the soap.

They also snuck around from classroom to classroom to look to see where hand sanitizer was located in the classrooms because we'd read some articles about how hospitals struggle—even doctors struggle with the same thing, of keeping their hands clean, and different things that

Figure 4.2. Students use an ultraviolet light to demonstrate the spread of germs from hand contact. (Photo: Brian Schultz)

hospitals have tried to do to try to encourage nurses and doctors to be more diligent about that. They snuck around to see where things were located and created this game around creating sanitation stations in each classroom, where they created mockups of classrooms on chart paper—with chairs and tables and different things. Students had to come in and create their own classroom—a sanitation station had to be part of their classroom. They also played the games when they had students come in.

They had each class come in over the course of several days, and presented each group with a PowerPoint. They did the sanitation station game. They did a thing where there was this powder that you put on your hands that will fluoresce under ultraviolet light and so they shook everybody's hands (see Figure 4.2). They had put the powder on their hands and shook everybody's hand as they walked in, and then at the end of the presentation went around and showed how the powder—as if that was germs, how that would spread.

Oh! There was also another component of it. One of the things that we had talked about was trying to—I don't know how we came across this, but it was this idea of how can we integrate some sort of challenge that was like the—

Brian Schultz: ALS water challenge.

Will Hudson: Yeah, and wanting to create something along those lines.

Brian Schultz: The water bucket challenge.

Will Hudson: Right, to challenge people to wash their hands and maybe to raise money in some capacity or do something along those lines. They did find—the students did a lot of research. We looked at five, six different organizations. Then it was like, "Okay, well, let's tie that in to the bigger project. What can we do that's really localized here in our community but also can connect and maybe have some sort of impact in communities in, ideally, some of the West African countries that we've studied?"

They had very specific criteria, which was really great. Whatever organization they were looking for, they wanted the organization to work in West Africa, to have something to do with health, and to focus on children. They felt like that was important, that it needed to be child-centric.

Brian Schultz: What was the challenge?

Will Hudson: They found an organization called The Water Project, which they really liked. One of the things they really liked about it is that you could create your own website. They gave you a template. Also, the organization would keep you updated as to where your money was going and the impact that it made in the different situations. It also dealt with health and water by providing access to water.

We talked about—one thing that I had to push was, "Why?" How do you connect access to clean water to sickness and death, or health? You've got to be able to make that connection. It went back to—it circled back around to, "Well, if you have access to clean water and know about waterborne diseases and stuff like that, you're going to have less chance of getting sick because of waterborne diseases." Also, if you're not sick all the time, that also will potentially give you—you'll be able to go to school. If you're not sick all the time, you're better positioned to pursue an education or whatever educational opportunities are being provided wherever you live.

Brian Schultz: They challenged the broader school community to do what in order to raise money? There's that piece of it. It's not just a matter of giving because we have and they don't—the important tension between charity and change. That is really the social justice part of the project. It's not just about charity, right?

Will Hudson: Right. I think that's this—that, to me, seems like this ongoing tension with these types of things, especially with the more affluent-type community that we have, is that it's really easy to throw money at stuff. I was comfortable with them doing some sort of trying to raise money as part of a larger awareness campaign. If it had just been that, if that had just been the project, I wouldn't have been as comfortable with that.

They were challenging people to drink just water for 3 weeks. Whenever they would go out to eat and stuff like that, they would have—instead of ordering soda or milk or whatever, they would have just water. Then whatever money they saved by not drinking pop or something like that, that was money that at the end of 3 weeks, they could then donate.

They really got behind that, too. It was funny to listen to them having the conversations among themselves, like, "Well, can I drink—I have a pop at the house that we bought before the challenge started. Can I drink that? Is that allowed?" "It's mostly water." Really, who was doing the challenge?

They really bought into it. It just lent itself to this heightened awareness of the water that they were using, the amount of money that they were throwing at one thing, whereas maybe that money could be directed toward others. Then I think another piece of it as well is that creating that awareness of not taking it for granted as much. We just take it for granted you can turn on the tap and you can have this water you can drink, and it won't make you sick, and that's not necessarily the norm in the rest of the world or in other parts of the world.

Brian Schultz: It seems like there's a lot of barriers or obstacles that came through this project. You discussed earlier the idea of culturing bacteria and controlling variables or even determining how they were going to take action and make the turn from a topically generated idea like sickness and death to then effecting change in the community. Now you're talking about this idea of how you interpret the challenge that they actually named and created in the first place.

One thing about doing these sorts of social action–oriented projects is that there are lots of barriers and obstacles that the teacher can't predict. How do you help students negotiate barriers to overcome them or help them to work around them?

LETTING STUDENTS LEAD AND SPINNING THE PLATES

Will Hudson: For me, going through it with them, it was always this challenge for me of—I talked about spinning the plates. There were so many things going on that they had never done before, and that they didn't have a whole lot of context for, that it was this constant of trying not to have my own ideas of what they could do, and also not knowing what they could do. It's this constant, just this ongoing idea of trying to stay two or three steps ahead of them at all times but then also, at the same time, not really knowing where they were going. I was having to pick and choose, trying to be really comprehensive in the preparation I was doing for myself, recognizing that maybe one track that I might go on as an individual, they might not go on that track. I'd have to shift gears to meet them where they were at throughout the project.

I think the biggest obstacle from start to finish—I think the first obstacle was just identifying the problem, moving them out of this very topic-oriented approach to having them just start thinking about their community and their place in it and what they can do to effect change or what they can do just to make things better in their own lives.

This was especially the case with the survey. They'd never done it before. It was all new. Just the languaging about it, spending a week just writing the survey itself, arguing and wrestling over certain words and phrases, and then thinking about who our audience was as well. Who were we writing this for?

Then distributing the survey. That was another thing. When we were going to distribute the survey, we realized that we couldn't just hand a survey to kindergartners and 1st-graders. How were we going to deal with that?" We had to constantly be thinking about who we were talking to. They talked to all the teachers and asked them what they would prefer. Would they prefer for them to come in and sit down with their students individually and go through the survey individually? Then there were the other classes that were comfortable just taking the survey as is. Especially on that one, every step of the way it was some decision that had to be made about how they were going to do it. I don't think there was a component of it that did not require some sort of a debate.

I think that was the biggest, a constant obstacle that was always there. Maybe that's what it is. You're creating this space for these kids. You're saying, "Okay, here's this space where you're able to make decisions about something that is important to you and you're able to make decisions and to do something. As your teacher, I'm telling you, basically, that I will support you in whatever decision you make. The one thing I'm not going to do is I'm not, within reason, going to make those decisions for you." You have them moving forward as a group into uncharted waters—one of the students said it was even scary. Not intimidating, but it's going out and putting themselves out there far into the community. So much of it was the dialogue that we had, this ongoing dialogue. "Well, what do we do next?" "Well, what do you think we should do next?"

Brian Schultz: One of those things that came up that wasn't necessarily a part of the original plan but was one of those "What do we do next?" pieces was the idea of bringing an expert in to stain slides and understanding how when you culture bacteria, how then you can examine it with microscopes. Maybe you could speak to that.

Will Hudson: Right. That's this funny thing. When do I make a decision as a teacher, saying, "We're going to do this"? I think that's this idea of looking at the scenario and saying, "Okay, they're doing this." Culturing the bacteria, we would be remiss if we didn't do—if we didn't do this other thing. If we didn't take it to the next level, it wouldn't be—

Brian Schultz: A missed opportunity, perhaps?

Will Hudson: Yeah. That's the thing. Where are the opportunities within this? There was a parent that had a lot of experience, had worked in a lab and had done Gram staining on bacteria, which is something I didn't have any experience with. It was really great to be able to have her come in and show them how to do this. Then it led us into this whole other tangent about bacteria and molecular biology.

Then it became this deal with me finding resources and going, "Okay, here are some resources. I want you to read these resources. I want you to be able to talk intelligently with me 5 days from now about bacteria," and then trying to couch it in terms of evolutionary theory and survival of the fittest and natural selection and all of these—

Brian Schultz: The connection's back, again, to West Africa.

Will Hudson: Exactly, and then being able to differentiate between what we're talking about, Ebola. Let's be really clear. Ebola is not a bacterium. Ebola is a virus. They're two very different things. Then even pushing them a little bit, saying, "Okay, well, you did these bacteria cultures. We can see the amount of bacteria we grew. How is that limited? What's the limitation with that?" And then the students had to come up with the notion that, "Well, we're limited in the fact that we can't culture viruses." We don't know. We have to infer. We have to make this inference based on what we're seeing and what we can observe to what we can't observe.

Brian Schultz: The project goes on for multiple months.

Will Hudson: Yeah, it would not end.

It's never-ending. Then there I was—it always came back to the survey, right? There was all this peripheral stuff. We had done everything. They had brought in the students from the classrooms. Then there's this question of the parents. They had shared their website and all of their stuff with the entire school community—the board of directors, the parents of every grade level—drumming up support for this.

Then there was this question about there not being a presentation for the parents. So we were like, "Okay. Now we've got to set that whole thing up." Then they did that. Then they contacted parents individually. We had support from other people who contacted other people from the community to come in. Then they did that. They did a great presentation to the parents. It was a great turnout (see Figure 4.3).

The project wouldn't die. At that point, I was more than happy for them to be done. There had been discussion of the follow-up survey and how that—they knew that. They understood that a follow-up survey was an important component of doing something like this. At that point, I would have been content with just knowing that a follow-up survey was an integral component; I probably would have been fine just to move off, but they wouldn't have it.

Then there was this really magical moment where all of a sudden there was this shift that occurred, where now the students were dragging me along. Like anything, there were probably times throughout the project where I was like, "Come on. We have to do this thing." They came along with me because it just had to get done. Then it just turns. I'm sitting here going, "Oh, my God. We're still doing this?"

They were dead-set on it. It had to be done. It kept going for an extra couple of weeks. They didn't really revise their survey, but they went and they printed off copies. They went and interviewed all the students that needed to be interviewed again. They sent them [the surveys] to the classrooms that had taken them independently again, brought it back, went through all the data, had a whole array of charts and figures, and then sat down, added the changes to their spreadsheet that was ongoing on their website.

We had this really great discussion about calculating percent of change, but then realizing as we were—spent about half an hour, 45 minutes on working with the figures—that there was this problem in

Figure 4.3. Students in Mr. Hudson's class engage with classroom visitors about their bacteria cultures. (Photo: Brian Schultz)

that the first time, we had interviewed about 100 students. The second time, we were only able to get 88. We had to accommodate for this in doing our calculations and figuring out what the percent of change was between the beginning survey and the end survey.

Brian Schultz: I gather from the fact that you were saying that if they hadn't done this essential post-test, if you will, you would have been okay with it. I am curious. Did their awareness campaign actually have any influence on the local community?

Will Hudson: It seems like it did. If the data are correct, there were areas that—they could see pretty marked improvement, especially with washing hands after blowing noses and coughing there was a fairly substantial improvement. Then the other one that they saw was this peripheral thing that occurred that was really interesting. They had a question about do you wash your hands more during cold and flu season. In the original survey, I don't know, it was maybe 40% or 30% said, "Yes, we wash our hands more," where in the follow-up survey, it was 60, 70%. They had this really large increase in an area that they hadn't even really focused on that dramatically.

It was interesting that it was just by proxy. By doing this one thing, we actually affected the way people were thinking about things during this time of the year. Once that was complete, they were able to wash their hands of it and to move on.

That was great. That was a really exciting—that was one of those moments you get—it is really exciting because it's theirs. It's not mine any longer, if ever it was. Whatever hands I had on the wheel at that point were off. They were steering that ship. That was pretty cool, to see that degree of ownership and creating a lot of work for themselves. It's not like it was just checking some—it was a lot of work, a lot of numbers. You had 100 kids and 10 questions per survey that were rated on a five-point Likert scale.

SUSTAINING EMERGENT CURRICULUM AND TRANSFERRING SKILLS

Brian Schultz: Any other sentiments that you want to share? What is your own takeaway from this project as a teacher?

Will Hudson: I think the question that I have for myself is how I can—keeping it going. How can you do this? Project after project, year after year? That's the ongoing question for me in this emergent setting. Can you expect every project to have this? Can you expect this every year or is this just a flash in the pan? I don't think that's a question I can really answer—I guess that's experiential.

Brian Schultz: Sure, but one of the things that I observe in your story and the experience is the tools that the students are learning along the way, which certainly had to do with the Localizing Ebola Project, are skills and techniques for participation and engaging in community change that can be transferable to many other situations or other problems that they want to solve or things they want to tackle.

Will Hudson: Well, that's interesting. One thing is since we've done that, I think that the students got a taste for it. The project that we're working on right now, there's this question that is very topical. We're studying music and sound. The students are saying, "Well, there has to be some sort of community outreach. There has to be this component of it."

I think they have that—they see that now, the project is not robust if we don't have this element. That's really exciting to see. One thing we talked about was imagining doing a political campaign or any type of campaign, where you're dealing with thousands and thousands of people, or something that's in a state or a nation, the amount of work that goes into it.

I think now they have this frame of reference for themselves. Will they use the very same tools? Perhaps, but they do have that experience. This is the process. It's slow and it's arduous. Choosing your words and all of these components of it. They got really fired up about fracking. This coming week, they're going to have a debate on the pros and cons of fracking. What's interesting about that is that we have students who are now doing research. They're finding these hydraulic fracturing companies, and they're sending them emails.

They're real savvy about it now. They're saying, "Oh, we're very interested in the process. Could you give us more?" Another student was calling up and ended up talking to the senior vice president of this one company, who ended up coming back and sending all this information about their operation. You do see this confidence to push, to get out there, and to start asking the questions and contacting people and other organizations and wanting to wrestle with these issues.

CHAPTER 5

The Sustainable Democracy Project
In Partnership with the Community

There are multiple ways to envision social action curriculum projects and teach in the cracks. Teachers at The Children's School and Jennifer McSurley in a neighborhood elementary school approach developing curriculum with students by looking directly to the young people as key classroom stakeholders that are afforded opportunities to co-develop teaching and learning. By encouraging the students themselves to identify topics of interest and issues of importance in their daily lives, the teachers in these instances leverage the children's ideas as curricular starting points.

The previous examples demonstrate the power of inverting the curriculum—a way of using the needs, wants, ideas, questions, and curiosities of students as a practical beginning to then allow curriculum to emerge and be created together. Using those young people's curiosities and questions led the groups of students alongside their teachers to engage in curriculum that transcended typical subject-matter or discipline-specific categorization and became emergent, holistic, integrated, powerful teaching and learning opportunities.

What is at the heart of these examples is the use of the confluence of student interest with the questions students have about the world. Reflective of the prompts that William Ayers (2004) encourages educators to consider with their students in *Teaching Toward Freedom*: "Who in the world am I? What place is this? What will become of me here? What larger universe awaits me? What shall I make of what I've been made? What are my choices?" (p. 33), the essence of these questions provides a means to develop meaningful, worthwhile curriculum in the classroom. Because students deem the topics important, this approach lends itself readily to creating classrooms that encourage critical thinking and problem solving through social activism, community engagement, and justice-oriented teaching and learning. The hook is built in and curriculum generates intrinsic motivation. Whereas the previous examples are powerful in their own right, there are other approaches to developing emergent curricula with students that foster engagement in social action curriculum projects.

BUILDING SUSTAINABLE DEMOCRACY AT PACHS

One such approach to developing curriculum projects rooted in community problems can be seen at the Dr. Albizu Campos Puerto Rican High School (PACHS) in the Humboldt Park neighborhood of Chicago. PACHS, a Chicago public school that is also part of the Youth Connection Charter Schools, is a founding member of the Alternative High School Network, a nonprofit member-based organization that seeks to partner with communities to help mitigate the extreme dropout crisis in Chicago, particularly in historically marginalized communities of color. Located in the predominantly Puerto Rican neighborhood commonly referred to by insiders as Paseo Boricua (which translates in English as Puerto Rican walk or promenade), most of the students attending PACHS have either dropped out or been pushed out of their neighborhood high schools. PACHS serves a very clear and defined need in educating students who otherwise might simply add to the growing dropout statistics of students in urban schools. The school is purposeful in its design: small class sizes; dedicated, caring teachers and staff; relevant and responsive curriculum; and wrap-around services such as on-site child care.

There is much to celebrate about PACHS. Many other educators and scholars have written extensively about PACHS and its deep potential for meeting the needs of students who otherwise have been dismissed by the system. This scholarship includes the powerful work of critical pedagogues René Antrop-González (2006, 2011) and Jason Irizarry (Irizarry & Antrop-González, 2007), where they describe the "school as sanctuary." This sanctuary frame encompasses a learning community where there are critical caring relationships between teachers and students, and the school itself is affirming of students' race and ethnicity. The school also works to provide spaces that are safe zones free of gangs. This, in part, can be attributed to the school not tolerating students throwing gang signs or wearing color representations of affiliation. Although students could be written up for such actions, the school leveraged mentors to speak with students who were gang members about the need for keeping the school free of gang associations so that it could be a safe space for all its students and staff.

All the studies done about PACHS point to the power in and the potential of a school that meets the students where they are, honors who they are and from where they come, and works in collaboration with the community. Other research about the community in which PACHS is located focuses on an asset-based and funds of knowledge perspective: Laura Ruth Johnson (2008, 2009) studies transformational family literacy, and Nilda Flores-González

(2001, 2002) writes on identity development of Latino students and the dropping out/pushing out of high school students in Paseo Boricua.

The focus of interest in this book is on how the school enacts curriculum with students—students who have fallen through the proverbial cracks of a large urban school system. In recent available data, Chicago Public Schools documented only a shameful 66.3% graduation rate—an entire third of the students who start 9th grade do not complete 12th grade (Vevea, 2015). In a challenge to the trope related to this dire situation, during the junior and senior high school years at PACHS, teachers and school leaders structure a multiple-month-long learning opportunity for its students to work together on projects they individually select based on presentations given by community organizations. Called the Sustainable Democracy Project (SDP), this curricular endeavor serves as a capstone project that challenges students to get involved in local issues.

The pedagogical intent of the SDP is to have the students see that they may use their voices in purposeful ways to speak out about and take action on issues that matter to them and injustices in their community. Not only is it necessary to have students matriculate through high school at significantly higher rates, but the school sees its mission as the creation of critical, engaged citizens who may effect change in their communities. Knowing that so many of the students have experienced school through the commonplace deficit perspective that blames the young people for society's inadequacies, the school sees the SDP as one opportunity for students to challenge this external and internalized perspective.

It is through purposeful scaffolding and subsequent hands-on activities that students are able to learn and practice ways to take action. These experiential opportunities can lead to students seeing themselves as change agents. No longer is school the means to further marginalize the students, but instead it is quite the contrary: a caring place where students feel safe, empowered, and challenged to see the world differently and then act on it. In this way, PACHS embodies what John Dewey (1907) called for in *The School and Society*, where each school could model a "miniature community, an embryonic society" (p. 32) so that students learn what it means to be an engaged citizen. This curricular stance at PACHS demonstrates the power of the tenets of progressive education. Not only is the curriculum reflective of society in that the projects in which students engage are actual pressing issues that community organizations have named as important, but the organizations have invited students to help them solve such social problems through activities and interest- or need-based initiatives (see Tozer & Senese, 2012). The SDP provides for a reciprocal relationship between the school and the community that echoes how and why the school was founded, while challenging the more typical unidirectional relationships often seen between schools and organizations. PACHS sees the students as change agents and structures the school to allow for practicing and enacting such agency. It is through this re-envisioning of what it means to be a student in the community that PACHS shows the power of the interrelationship of students, teachers, and community.

But rather than looking directly to the students to name issues and problems in the community that they would like to solve, as other teachers and schools have done and as has been documented in previous chapters, PACHS takes a unique and purposeful approach to identifying topics for study and engagement. Partnering and in solidarity with community-based organizations and agencies, some of which were the very impetus for the school's founding over 40 years ago, PACHS provides students with real-world challenges and opportunities to help solve authentic community problems—actual issues that are happening at this very moment in the Paseo Boricua/ Humboldt Park neighborhood.

AGITATING STUDENTS

To introduce this challenge to students, PACHS's then-principal, Matthew Rodríguez, created a video that presented the broad idea of the Sustainable Democracy Project and his call to action for the students. While Principal Rodríguez had daily interactions with most students at school, he chose to make a video that students could use as a resource and refer to as they worked through their projects and contingent action planning. In addition, a video presentation allowed for the young women students who were on maternity leave at the time to have full access to the prompt. The following is a transcript of that video orientation:

> Hello. My name is Matthew Rodríguez and I'm the proud principal of Albizu Campos Puerto Rican High School.
>
> If you did not know, this year we are celebrating our school's 40th anniversary. I want to share a little bit about where our school comes from and where I hope we can go.
>
> In the beginning, our school was created after a report came out called the Lucas Report. This report identified that 73.9% of Puerto Rican students were dropping out of the Chicago public school system.
>
> Many people looked at this figure and said that the reason why students were dropping out, particularly from Chicago Public Schools,

was because those students were lazy. They didn't care about their education. Their families didn't care about their education.

Many community activists in the Puerto Rican community said that there was something else that was happening. Something else was wrong and needed to be resolved.

What they believed was that the Chicago public school system and [what was] happening in there were all manifestations of 21st-century racism.

In the end, what they did was that they got together; they identified, obviously, what the problem was; they put a plan and a strategy together about how they could resolve that problem; and their solution, which they implemented, is the school that you currently attend right now—Dr. Pedro Albizu Campos Puerto Rican High School.

When our school was created, it was built not for students only to learn about their history and their culture. Not for students only to learn about what it means to be a high school graduate. What it meant was that students would be able to take what they learned and implement it in making positive social change in their community. That they would be agitated to the point that they'd want to do something. Take responsibility for the challenges that they encounter and do something about it in their community.

Over the years, since the beginning of the school, I've noticed—and I've been principal for 5 years and I've been in this school for 10 years—I've seen, slowly, that students are less and less involved with positive social change. Positive social transformation. Less and less involved with the community that our school is situated in.

I have a challenge that I'd like to pose to the student body at Albizu Campos. That challenge is for you to be proponents of sustainable democracy. What it means is for you to actualize our school's mission and vision that talk about self-determination, self-actualization, and self-reliance.

What it means is for you to hear from some of our community members the challenges that our community is facing. It means for you to identify clearly what those challenges mean and what the consequences are if those challenges are not provided a solution.

It means that I want you guys to get together and identify different ways that you think solutions can be implemented in our community. It means that I want you to take responsibility for those solutions and implement them in our community. Collect data and determine whether or not it's a viable solution.

It means that I want you to become active citizens in this neighborhood, which is ultimately what sustainable democracy is all about.

I hope that you take the time to really listen carefully to the community leaders that you're getting ready to hear from and that you come up with the best solutions that you can possibly imagine, implementing all the skills that you are learning in all your classes.

In the end, I hope that you make our school proud. I hope that you make our school's founders proud in the 40th-year anniversary.

Thank you.

The SDP itself is reflective of the ethos of the school. As Principal Rodríguez notes, PACHS was founded in the 1970s in response to the deficit narrative that the extremely low rates of high school graduation for children in the Humboldt Park community were because they were too lazy and did not care about their education. This all too common characterization of disinterested and apathetic youth from historically marginalized communities has persisted in many large urban school districts since the school opened. PACHS's raison d'etre, then, can be viewed as a response to schools that lack both cultural relevance and responsiveness to the communities they serve. The complex relationship between the school and the community, and therefore the SDP itself, also is rooted in the broader historical legacy of the Puerto Rican people's struggle for self-determination. Indeed, as Antrop-González (2011) argues, echoing one of the student participants in his research on PACHS, the school has the potential, if not the promise, to be a "radical sanctuary" honoring students for their culture and ethnicity and caring for them in meaningful ways. This is illustrated, for example, in the school's deliberately accommodating students who were on maternity leave. Part of this caring also means challenging the students to become more wide-awake, to respond to pressing issues in the community, and to take purposeful action.

As Principal Rodríguez noted in his orientation to students, students have become less involved since the inception of the program. This may be a result of a variety of contextual factors, including the marginalization of voices, particularly of youth of color in and around Chicago; the overreliance on culturally and racially biased test scores; and the upsurge in violence in the city. A host of other factors that allowed less time for community engagement also contributed to the reduced involvement, including everything from homelessness, familial responsibilities after school, and the need for child care for students with children. In addition, many students traveled from neighborhoods outside of Paseo Boricua, and those who were in the community rarely deviated from a specific route to and from school for safety concerns. Other students transferred to PACHS and may have not connected with community issues as part of their previous schooling experiences.

And yet, despite all of these mitigating circumstances, the school continues to see promising aspects for both students and community. PACHS's unique curricular approach in seeking sustainable democracy can be seen as a manifestation of Jeffrey Duncan-Andrade's (2009) definition of critical hope in his acclaimed *Harvard Educational Review* article, "Note to Educators: Hope Required When Growing Roses in Concrete." Principal Rodríguez celebrates Duncan-Andrade's thesis, referred me to it, and suggested the school's agreement to these ideas in having responsibility to foster, as he put it, "the ability to control one's destiny," and to engender this conviction in students. As Rodríguez contends, "The Sustainable Democracy Project is one piece to the puzzle of taking learning to a level of meaning and relevance . . . so that students directly apply school to transforming their lives." In addition to having this frame for learning, Rodríguez shared with me that he saw part of his role as "leading staff to increase their efficacy and understanding of how their work in a classroom can and must have larger implications for the surrounding community." It is in these ways that Sustainable Democracy Projects have their transformational capacity.

What sets PACHS apart is how it embodies a mission that centers its existence on continuously working to solve social problems related to community issues. The school itself is an exemplar of a social action curriculum project. This work not only is reflective of the school itself, but also is how the school seeks to develop curriculum with students and the community on an ongoing basis. Many of the scholars who have written about PACHS for other purposes, highlight the reflection of Paulo Freire's (1970/2000) ideas in how the school is both conceived and enacted. In addition to clearly creating ways to engage in praxis and developing conscientiousness among students, the school framework embodies John Dewey's educational philosophy. In thinking about how these underpinnings come alive, I am reminded of the argument that William Schubert (2006) detailed in an *Education and Culture* article. In the essay, Schubert discusses a strategy he learned from a former student for interpreting John Dewey's contributions to the field of education wherein the dualistic "and" in the titles of Dewey's books can be swapped for the word "is." The book titles can then be seen as the central argument of each volume wherein the words can be used both reflexively and interchangeably. In this way, PACHS is an example of carrying out a Deweyan call to action as described in *The School and Society* (1907), *Democracy and Education* (1916), or *Experience and Education* (1938). The school is representative of society, and society/the community embodies the ideas inherent in the school. PACHS's work within the Sustainable Democracy Project can be understood in this way as it relates to experience and education—the projects push students to see the interconnectedness of what are seemingly simple or disparate ideas.

In looking to community-based organizations that are trying to solve pressing issues in the neighborhood, the PACHS curriculum moves away from abstract ideas to concrete, specific, and relevant ones. Actual people working in the community organizations come to the school or write a letter to the student body presenting the problem with which they are grappling. So often schooling is relegated to distant concepts and ideas; the SDP rejects those commonplace practices and features topics that are responsive to the issues to which many students are readily connected. There is no prescriptive nature of the topics.

PICKING THE PROJECT

Part of PACHS's vision is to position students as community partners who work collaboratively with agencies and organizations to address critical social issues. This does not happen by accident. In fact, the PACHS faculty make a concerted, purposeful effort to engage in problem-posing education themselves. For instance, Principal Rodríguez pointed out to me that he and his faculty read Freire together, and "unpacked what it meant to engage a 'generative theme.'" In Rodríguez's words, it is important that "teachers and principals do not determine those, [but] they become skilled at deciphering them." Based on this engagement with one another, PACHS faculty invite the community-based organizations to pitch or propose projects to the students. This pitching can take different forms; for instance, the representatives have made short video presentations or written letters.

The students individually vote on the issue that best reflects their own interests, questions, and curiosities. In addition to empowering students as decisionmakers, this process requires them to prioritize competing ideas and think strategically about how to maximize their impact. After selecting a project, students then work with teachers and community representatives to plan a course of action. The course of action takes different forms for different causes, but is meant to lead students to develop research acumen and analysis skills, think about root causes of issues, and subsequently take action to solve a problem at hand. Because the community organizations' missions typically relate to the problem they are bringing to students' attention, the representatives are great resources in pointing the students in the right direction to learn more about the topics they present. This offers a starting point for student research about the issue and related topics.

At PACHS, the pitch process begins in the summer, long before the students enter the classroom for the year. As a dynamic, authentic project, the process varies from year to year according to an array of contextual factors, including the specific faculty involved, current community issues, and any priorities that have arisen at the school. However, the following is illustrative of how the process typically unfolds. A former senior portfolio and English teacher, Elizabeth Hoffman, discussed partnership opportunities with Principal Rodríguez based on the emergent themes identified by the broader faculty. Topics included issues ranging from youth violence, sexually transmitted diseases, access to safe and reliable public transformation, to high unemployment among young people and food deserts. Between the two of them and their various networks in the community, they determined potential partners. This list included everyone from contacts within established community organizations to friends, colleagues, and even downstairs neighbors. From there, Elizabeth and Principal Rodríguez met during the summer with each of the potential partners to discuss the school's priorities related to the project, using the previous year as a framework to work out kinks and think through scheduling.

Because the school was founded with input from various community institutions to meet the needs of the neighborhood, the school has many partnerships already in place. PACHS collaborates with various groups because it, too, has become a hallmark of the community. Once the partners have committed to participating in a project, the organizations visit the students, film a video, or write letters to the students outlining their needs and the problems they are trying to resolve. This is how the students and their community mentors from the various organizations begin to develop positive relationships. Schools wanting to initiate a program like that at PACHS might cultivate local partners by looking to advocacy organizations already connected to the school, or to community or nonprofit organizations already doing work to improve the area in which the school is located.

Teachers involved in the SDP utilize a framework drawn from problem-based learning (PBL). The school provided teachers with related professional development through the Illinois Math and Science Academy (IMSA), a recognized leader in STEM-related teaching practices and teacher resources related to inquiry and imagination. Elizabeth integrated materials from IMSA, particularly ideas from the PBL Tool Kit (2012), into her work with students. Elizabeth notes that "using the PBL outline helped ground the often-fluctuating process of SDP," but she also contends that framing the curriculum in this way made "the SDP 'official' in the eyes of YCCS [Youth Connection Charter School—the organization that holds the PACHS charter—a charter operator that serves at-risk youth and focuses on addressing high dropout rates among Chicago's African American and Latino youth] and implementation of the Common Core." The Tool Kit can be a resource for any school or teaching team that wants to legitimize initiation of such a project to its administration.

THE SUSTAINABLE DEMOCRACY PROJECT

To characterize how the students are introduced to an issue, the following is an invitation from the school's former assistant principal and director of urban agriculture, Mr. Carlos DeJesús. In the invocation, Mr. DeJesús describes how the school, in partnership with the Puerto Rican Cultural Center (PRCC)—an organization that has a long and complex history with PACHS and oversaw the school in its early years—can address the needs of the community. In his challenge to the students, he focuses on how the neighborhood is considered a food desert, identified as a geographic area in which it is difficult to obtain fresh produce or nutritious food. In what was his dual role with both PACHS and PRCC, Mr. DeJesús outlines a challenge for the students to engage in authentic problem solving.

My name is Carlos DeJesús. I'm assistant principal at Albizu Campos High School. I'm also the director of urban agriculture for a collaboration between the high school and the Puerto Rican Cultural Center.

This is something that we've been working on, really, for the past 6 years. Our community has been designated a food desert. It doesn't mean that we don't have food. It means that we don't have nutritious food. It's difficult for us to be able to buy a tomato. In some cases, we would have to leave the community in order to do so.

Part of the issue of a food desert is that there's an overabundance of high-fat and high-calorie food, but that's very low in nutrition. There's also an overabundance of fast food.

This has caused a real problem for our community, as it happens in almost all food deserts, because that leads to obesity. Obesity is the gateway for a bunch of other problems, like diabetes and high blood pressure and high cholesterol and heart disease and stroke. In too many of our families, it ends up causing death.

We, at the school, have been trying to work at this. One of the things that we did was that 6 years ago, a group of students got together and came up with ideas on how to resolve the food desert. What they came up with was the idea of establishing the urban agriculture program that has resulted, in part, in this beautiful greenhouse that we have here. It's a unique feature of the school. We use it to help students learn how to grow food.

Now, one of the challenges is that we have yet to grow anywhere near as much food as we want. We have established something called the Sofrito Project, where students are learning to grow all of the ingredients of sofrito. That's a really wonderful thing. It's really been an excellent learning experience. The things that we start to grow here, we take to the community gardens. We haven't grown enough food. Certainly, nowhere near enough to be able to help meet the needs of the community.

The challenge for you is to help us figure out how to expand the urban agriculture program. How to make it so that we can produce the quantities of food that we need.

Last year, we produced about 600 pounds of produce. Mostly tomatoes and green peppers and cucumbers, but not very much by way of sofrito. What we would want to do is to increase that number significantly. If we can double the amount this year and double it again the next year, that would be truly fantastic.

The challenge for you is to help us make that determination. Figure out how we can improve how we use the greenhouse and the gardens, so that we can really make a dent in the food desert. I know that this can be done, because these—this wonderful idea of an urban agriculture program came from students just like you, having this sort of exercise, where you're working together to research an issue in the community and come up with solutions.

That's the challenge for you. I know that you can do this. Help us out.

Students at PACHS readily would understand Mr. DeJesús's reference to sofrito and the necessary ingredients. For readers who are not familiar with sofrito, the ingredients include a mixture of different kinds of peppers, onions, tomatoes, garlic, and cilantro that makes up a base used in many Puerto Rican foods. For his community, sofrito would represent sufficient ingredients for a healthy culturally valued diet. Figure 5.1 shows the PACHS rooftop greenhouse.

Figure 5.2 presents additional examples of how community-based organizations or advocacy groups propose a project or related challenge to the PACHS students. In each of the letters, an executive director or other key stakeholder describes the mission of the organization and the work that it does, identifies critical issues of concern to the organization, and subsequently outlines a campaign or task in which the students may engage. If and as

Figure 5.1. The PACHS rooftop greenhouse, where the vegetables for sofrito are cultivated by students. (Photo: Brian Schultz)

appropriate, the letter includes information about potential partners, suggestions, and potential action steps that the organization has identified to help the students move the project forward.

Like any successful social action curriculum project, the SDP relies on a constellation of school- and community-based factors, including a supportive administration, effective school–community partnerships, and committed educators. Elizabeth Hoffman's creativity, flexibility, and passion for fostering engaging and empowering learning experiences enabled her to adapt to students' interests and meet community-based organizations' needs, all while responding to the emergent nature of the curriculum.

Elizabeth is one of those amazing teachers who clearly works hard to build strong relationships with her students. And this is a quite a feat at PACHS, since most of the students have been pushed out of other schools for a multitude of reasons, ranging from attendance and truancy to behavior or teen pregnancy. Elizabeth did this by working to build trust among her students in multiple ways. From encouraging students to question her or developing rules and expectations together, to sharing her personal phone number with them, Elizabeth consistently looked for ways to nurture the often-complex relationships with students. As a guest in her classroom, I could see how Elizabeth cultivated a community of trust, as she worked to

Figure 5.2. Community-based organizations' letters to PACHS students related to the Sustainable Democracy Project. (Photo: Brian Schultz)

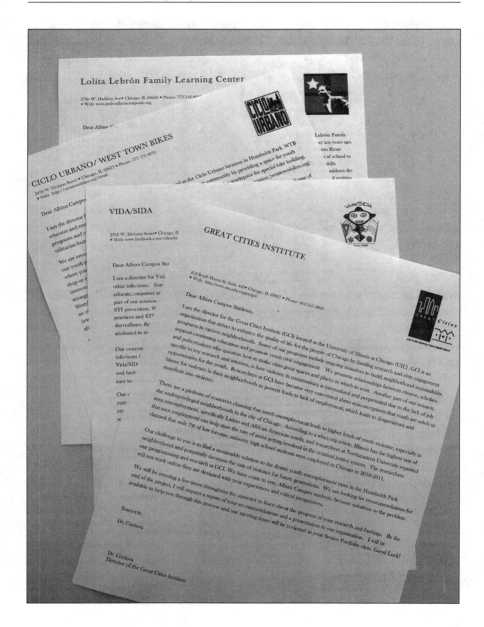

break down barriers of authority and created ways to develop mutual respect and a "more equal" playing field. Her many different strategies in her relational work with students were evident when I spent time in her classroom and when students defended their SDP portfolios to panels of "experts," in which I had been invited to participate, at the end of their senior year. Further, these connections were built over time and through interactions in and out of the classroom. Elizabeth lived in the community—literally just down the block from the school. This proximity allowed her to participate in community activities, call parents and make visits to students' homes, and tutor students after school. Clearly, Elizabeth saw herself as a member of the community. Whereas teachers living outside the communities in which they teach can find ways to get involved in activities and organizations that help them cultivate relationships with their students, in this case Elizabeth's students were not only aware of her community membership status, but also embraced it.

During a recent exchange about what contributed to the success of the school's Sustainable Democracy Project, Elizabeth articulated to me that it acted as

> a catalyst for students, teachers, and community members to become participants of a dynamic social transformation process together, developing problem-solving and critical-thinking skills together, and sharing an ever-expanding amount of creativity. The SDP highlighted the heart of what I believe teaching should invoke, student voice.

Beyond the importance of cultivating student voice, Elizabeth contended that students "became empowered by the SDP because their knowledge, experiences, and unique skill sets were centric to implementing solutions in their community. The students were being viewed as young intellectual activists who were needed and respected within the community."

Not only does Elizabeth see that students can be empowered by the Sustainable Democracy Project, but she argues that the SDP allowed her to develop as a teacher. The SDP created spaces for her to

> learn a tremendous amount about the community, the students, and myself. I became a better version of myself due to the consistent critique from students, community partners, and collaborating teachers. I absolutely loved standing back and observing the highly intellectual and critical conversations students were having with the community partner members. I loved creating a classroom where students schooled me, as it displaced the prevalent top-down learning dynamic. The SDP

allowed my classroom to be loud, engaging, intense, fun, and exciting. It was amazing to bask in the glow of the final presentations and share them with outside panelists.

PUSHING BEYOND THE PREDICTABLE

Whereas the SDP is clearly an example of powerful teaching and learning, and empowering in its ability to create a culturally responsive classroom space and excite teachers and students alike, the individual projects are not always easy or predictable. Part of the promise of social action curriculum projects is the necessity of overcoming obstacles, being pushed to the cusp of comfort zones, or beyond perceived limits. These potential barriers create situations that could become impediments that are hard to overcome.

In response to my questions about the challenges faced and the difficulties she overcame, Elizabeth articulated her annoyance, frustration, and contemplation by expressing some of the complexities that teaching within and through the Sustainable Democracy Projects created for her. Elizabeth needed to keep an eye toward an increasingly test-oriented culture. She also needed to communicate and cultivate relationships with partners, and develop and track assessments. This was in addition to the work necessary to help students maintain their portfolios, a school-based requirement for graduation, so the students could be successful in ultimately presenting their efforts to an external panel drawn from the neighborhood or broader Chicago area who had an interest in the Sustainable Democracy Projects or a vested interest in seeing the school's success in action. In Elizabeth's words:

It was so challenging to organize the Sustainable Democracy Project while simultaneously building an entire online portfolio with students. Some community partner mentors were more active and organized than others, which created inconsistencies. At times, I was more invigorated by the Sustainable Democracy Project and less with the portfolio process and really had to spend equal time with both aspects of the class and curriculum. At times, communication between the community partners, students, and me was complicated, which made me a better communicator but was also a source of frustration. I was perpetually frustrated with fighting for a social action/transformation curriculum among the ever-looming testing culture that was slowly lurking into the corners of PACHS. During the final presentation of the SDP there was always a debate about how to "properly" grade students' projects and learning processes. The rubric I used was an ever-changing debate among community partners, staff, and myself. Everyone had an opinion and I had to figure out what was the best for the students and me, and keep it in line with the history of PACHS. Many times, I doubted myself and my efforts because the SDP does not lend itself to immediate, quantifiable results of student improvement. . . . Student attendance was difficult sometimes because a missed day was a ton of missed information. Some days we were all lost in research and students became frustrated with not finding results and immediate solutions. I had to explain to them so many times that they were part of a larger solution and that they may not see changes immediately . . . rather, they were leaving a mark for the future group of seniors that would inherit the community problem.

Many teachers will be able to relate to the dilemmas Elizabeth faced in her classroom. Competing expectations related to the curriculum, in this case engaging in the Sustainable Democracy Project and developing the online portfolios, push teachers to negotiate what they have to do and what they believe is right for students. Student attendance issues disrupt the flow of curricular engagement. Pressures of high-stakes assessments are a constant distraction. Similarly, involving community members in school projects makes classroom interactions unpredictable in other ways: Some individuals have more time and attention to give, or some are better able to relate to students. All of the challenges Elizabeth articulates, and others she does not name, like pressures from the upper administration of the district or charter organizations, will have an effect on the experiences students and teachers alike face when pushing back on commonplace assumptions about how schools should be organized and the types of curricula that should be in classrooms.

These ideas are not lost on administrators either. Teachers need to make certain that when engaging in these curricular endeavors, they have the support of their administrators. In Elizabeth's case, she was in partnership from the beginning with her principal. In similar fashion, Principal Rodríguez reflected on how the entire PACHS approach presented obstacles, but the school's conviction in its approach and theoretical framework proved to be worthwhile. This conviction, in part, likely provided a vehicle for highlighting the power inherent in doing this kind of work with young people. In Rodríguez's words:

The persistent challenge that we faced as a school was that we were going against the grain on so many fronts. One example of our uphill battle is that we are situated in a culture of standardized testing as the only legitimate measure of student learning, casting doubt upon our more wholistic approach to students' demonstration of mastery. We were constantly questioned and ridiculed in relation to people's assumptions of the level of rigor that students experienced. What sent the doubters running is when our students would take the same standardized tests as every other student across the nation, and in many cases would outperform their counterparts. During the implementation of the SDP, we were able to move our school out of "probation" and into CPS's top rating of Tier 1+, a rating that is based on a measurement where 50% of the school's performance is based on students' performance on a standardized test.

Despite the setbacks from attendance to bigger picture ideas like getting the students to see themselves as change agents, Elizabeth and Matthew show the power and potential of this approach to curriculum. There is a lot to learn from the school's overall approach to engaging in Sustainable Democracy Projects, the support of and expectation from a principal like Matthew, and an individual teacher's practices, like those of Elizabeth. Teachers and administrators alike should find reassurance in seeing that approaching curriculum in such inventive, emergent ways also can yield results on more traditional forms of assessment. For teachers contemplating doing this kind of work with students and developing community partnerships, I hope the sentiments of a teacher and principal who were deeply committed to it, for all its rough edges and uncertainty, show that it not only can be accomplished, but can be accomplished with rich possibilities.

* * *

Since the time of the events described in this chapter, much has shifted at Dr. Pedro Albizu Campos Puerto Rican High School. Many changes at the school are related to or exacerbated by the financial crises associated with public education in Illinois. The interviews with the school personnel about the deep potential of the Sustainable Democracy Project that informed this chapter occurred after each practitioner had moved on from their roles within the school. Not surprisingly, though, they all remain focused on justice issues related to teaching and community in their current pursuits. Principal Rodríguez works for the nonprofit principal preparation program, New Leaders, developing transformational principals in Chicago and across the country. Carlos DeJesús oversees programs related to homelessness at the nonprofit Heartland Alliance. Elizabeth Hoffman relocated out of state and currently is seeking her teaching license so that she may return to the classroom. Although these and other changes have occurred, according to one of the school's previous principals and its current president of the board of directors, Marvin Garcia, "The mission of the school remains steadfast, and the work related to meeting the needs of the students and community continues." Garcia goes on to proudly articulate, "Although budget cuts have been challenging, and some leadership at Albizu has changed, the same commitments to building sustainable democracy endure."

CHAPTER 6

Becoming the Teacher I Want to Be

Finding Support to Teach in the Cracks

Given the current context of educational reform, I often am told by teachers that developing emergent curriculum that focuses on students' concerns is simply not possible. Either an administrator, they say, would never permit it. Or a teacher claims she cannot find the time, space, or opportunity to engage in such an approach to developing curriculum with her students. Some even go as far as saying, "How can I throw out the curriculum to do such projects with my students?" Aside from my having a different interpretation of curriculum than the latter individual, these sentiments, taken together, initially frustrate me. They remind me of the disturbing direction educational reforms have taken. The fact that teachers do not have enough autonomy to enact what I have called a "teacher vision"—the ideas, inclinations, attitude, and curriculum that teachers envision will do right by their students—is demonstrative of the very troubling times in which we find the educational field. But the fact is that these concerns are very real for many teachers in today's classrooms. What are teachers to do? Is it possible to turn toward students to construct curriculum when a particular context does not seem to permit it?

The ideas and examples throughout this book highlight teachers and even whole schools that are able to readily engage in the cracks to reach students in ways that are problem- and project-based and justice-oriented. Some find opportunities within or in spite of mandates and expectations, while others have an entire school mission or a storied history centered on exploiting openings to teach for justice or in democratic ways. However, the reality is that many teachers do not feel that they have the room to do so. They feel bombarded by standards, assessments, and evaluations. They feel their hands are tied. They feel forced to teach what the state, district, or school has determined is necessary for their students. In this predicament, these teachers constantly must negotiate between what they are told to do through prescriptive mandates and predetermined curricula, and what they know will connect and resonate with, and has the potential to transform, their students. And they ought to feel frustrated. The current moment is troubling at best.

What is a teacher to do when she finds herself having a philosophy of education and a teacher vision that do not necessarily align with a school's expectations? No doubt this is a precarious situation for any teacher. I encourage my preservice university students to find principals and administrators who share their philosophy and beliefs about the capacity of young people. But this is often not enough. The trouble is that even when teachers find those like-minded administrators, the pressures of today's classroom environments can still push teachers to feel as though they must succumb to demands from the outside while they engage with their students inside the classroom. The cracks in these contexts are much more narrow. The openings must rest within a more traditionally based curricular format. Lesson and unit plans are developed. Standards must align. Activities are preplanned. Assessments are predetermined. Walk-throughs. Checklists. Administrators watching. Visiting. Assessing. Evaluating.

This chapter highlights the ways in which two teachers find cracks within the context of more restrictive school and classroom environments while working in partnership with their schools' administrations. Both teachers rely heavily on organizations outside of their schools to help them enact powerful teaching and learning within their classrooms. The organizations, Facing History and Ourselves and Mikva Challenge, provide and support teachers with robust curricular materials and professional development. In this chapter, we see Milli Salguero and Jennifer McSurley (both coauthors of Chapter 3 in this book) championing justice-based, action-oriented teaching by looking for and getting support from these outside organizations. Milli, teaching in a dual-language middle school classroom in a K–8 public charter school, shows the power of leveraging Facing History and Ourselves. Jennifer, teaching middle-level grades in a K–8 neighborhood magnet-cluster public elementary school, demonstrates the deep potential of using frameworks from Mikva Challenge that were developed in partnership with her school district. Both Milli and Jennifer have strong and positive working relationships with their respective administrations, but organizations such as those detailed in this chapter can help other teachers who find themselves in more hostile environments to see possibilities and find openings for developing curricula that are responsive to their students.

FINDING WAYS TO CONNECT AMID THE HIGH STAKES

Milli Salguero is a teacher who has found a way to teach in the cracks within a school that takes district mandates and school reform initiatives very seriously. Her school is a public charter school that has a mission rooted in honoring the whole child. The school has been written about as a successful example of public progressive education that can be a model for other schools to emulate. The school also takes the testing of students and evaluation of teachers as a grave matter. The school strives not only to be in line with the best practices within its mission but also to realize this mission against the backdrop of high-stakes testing and mandates. In so doing, the school also embraces the outside expectations placed upon it by school reform champions. In turn, teachers must find ways to interpret these expectations as they formulate their plans for the classroom. Clearly supporting its teachers, the school offers coaching by master teachers, significant resources, and seemingly endless professional development opportunities for all its educators.

Whereas the hoop-jumping often associated with the reform movement may give many teachers pause, Milli is able to create a classroom environment where high expectations are a hallmark, students flourish and achieve, and relationships between the teacher and students continuously develop. A focus on this relational work, coupled with efforts to center the curriculum on young adolescent development and identity, is a cornerstone. Milli's personal vision of a democratic, emergent curriculum is challenged, though, by the fact that, in her words:

> I create my unit plans, generally 10–12 weeks long, in advance using a shared calendar format. Each day has a clear teaching objective and documentation about how I am going to show skill progression and assess mastery of each skill for each day. I document 10 weeks in advance the particular Common Core skills I am going to teach each day, what materials will be used, how I will assess these skills, and what cold texts (a text that students have not yet seen) I will use in the assessment. At the beginning of each unit, I have to know the direction of where the materials will be headed so that I can be prepared in advance. While I see the benefit of being planned out and organized and am supported by my administration with resources to do so, I also see missed opportunities for organic problem-based curriculum.

Milli's lessons are in fact detailed, extremely well planned out, and in the format designed by her school. For instance, one unit plan related to her study with students about the Cambodian Genocide was 15 pages long. Not only has she planned out the lessons, activities, essential questions, vocabulary, and assessments months in advance, but Milli also aligns the curriculum with the Common Core State Standards in both English and Spanish. Since she teaches at a dual-language school, the expectation is that she will design, develop, and translate all materials for her 5th- and 6th-graders in both languages. It should be noted, though, that Milli is not alone in having to preplan her lessons and units, as this approach is commonplace across the educational landscape in many schools today.

FACING HISTORY AND OURSELVES:
HELPING TO NAVIGATE THE MANDATES OR EXPECTATIONS

With the encouragement and support of her school, Milli leans heavily on many outside organizations to help her reach her students. Her favorite and the one that she utilizes most is the organization Facing History and Ourselves (FH). FH is a powerful educational advocacy organization that Milli leverages as a mechanism for finding the opening(s) for inquiry-based instruction and justice-oriented teaching and learning. Milli really does engage in innovative, rich curriculum with her middle school students in what some might consider a tougher, more restrictive environment—one that is all too common in our current context. The nonprofit and nonpartisan FH frames itself as an international educational and professional development organization dedicated to helping students disrupt racism, prejudice, and stereotypes to promote a more just society. This framing helps to create the openings and provide opportunities for Milli, as well as her administration, to feel good about integrating the FH lessons into her classroom.

The organization aligns its curricular materials and professional development with the Common Core State Standards and, more important, has the heft, reputation, personnel, vibrant history of doing strong work, and even marketing materials that a lone teacher does not have. Milli believes that the ideas and materials of FH are perfect catalysts in and for her teaching context. Not only does this entity give her teaching tools and resources for classroom use, but Milli also feels as though the organization provides backup, professional development, and clout with her school that gives her a sort of license or even permission to take on powerful teaching and learning that are culturally responsive and justice-oriented. Though Milli continually says that she is not yet the teacher she wants to be, this kind of organization helps. The organization also makes its materials available online for free and has lending libraries for classroom use. And, in a cash-strapped district, Milli's school comes up with the resources to consistently send her to professional development across the country sponsored by FH and other similar organizations.

Utilizing curriculum units and plans from FH, Milli has taught units on Identity and Community, the Cultural Revolution in China, and the Cambodian Genocide through the FH lens. These are just a small sampling of the content and topics in which Milli engages the young people in front of her. Whereas this version of the cracks is very different from the examples in previous chapters because of the pressures from mandates and expectations of raising test scores, some teachers need to employ such preplanned or prede- signed resources, and use more formulaic curricular materials that are flexible or scalable, to become the teachers they want to be and connect with their students. In Milli's words:

> I've been able to teach in the way that I have, through small cracks, because of organizations like FH, which my school fully supports. I am able to create intentional, meaningful, rigorous units. Through their wealth of resources, I've been able to guide my students through the FH scope and sequence and discover a whole new way of teaching and learning. The process starts with a study of the Individual and Soci- ety—this portion of each unit focuses on how individual and national identities are formed. This is a critical part of my teaching—it's where I'm able to really hook kids in because suddenly history is relevant to them when we start discussing their identities, their experiences, and their choices. We then continue to the We and They portion and dis- cuss how, historically, making choices about who is included and who is excluded has led to mass violence and social injustices. Again, another critical part of my teaching, as middle schoolers definitely can relate to the "in and out groups." We then dive into the historical case study, the legacy piece, and the choosing to participate piece. FH has entire units planned out using this scope and sequence—they also have resources for just about any historical event you can imagine. FH offers PD work- shops and seminars—I think I've attended all of them. My school truly believes in the FH model because it allows students to discover who they are and make connections between history and the choices they confront every day. FH has a lending library where they let you check out class sets of books, videos, teaching guides, etc. It is incredibly easy to get things from them, you always email or talk to a real person, and your program associate is always available with teaching ideas/sugges- tions. Teaching through FH makes getting into SACPs more seamless because kids have already been making connections between history and social issues around them. FH materials/units/lessons are CCSS aligned, which allows for the accountability piece to be scratched off the to-do list.

As noted in Milli's response to why FH is an asset to her teaching and her classroom, she sees the materials and the topics as a motivational hook for her students to engage in deep curricular exploration. Because of her exceptional use of and enthusiasm for the material, it should be no surprise that Milli was invited to be part of the local Facing History and Ourselves Teacher Leadership Team. The organization brings teachers together to discuss ideas, present new curricular units and resources, and get feedback from the educators who will be utilizing the materials in their classrooms. Milli finds that being part of this team has given her the opportunity to meet with other like-minded educators who also are wrestling with the current educational reform policies and who also are still shaping their identities as teachers. Milli's eagerness about being a part of this leadership team is palpable:

> We share our stories. We get vulnerable. And together we find even the tiniest cracks. Then we all go to school the following day and try the new ideas with our students. As teachers, we share the same struggle, and there's comfort in that because it shows me that I'm not totally crazy.

Milli sees this as a great opportunity in the coming school year as she transitions from teaching 5th- and 6th-graders to teaching 7th and 8th grades. I have visited her classroom, and this does seem like a perfect storm for Milli to do what she envisions. She explained:

> I'm working my way there. Right now I'm not teaching through social action projects, but I am teaching through a social justice–oriented lens. As a new(er) teacher, I still have to work around the parameters and learn how to really widen those cracks. This is work that I reflect on daily because it's the teacher identity I'm still trying to shape.

Milli is particularly excited about the next opportunities she will have with this leadership group, as she sees it as an entryway for digging deeper into doing more emergent social action curriculum projects with her students. Milli's articulation of her action-oriented teaching philosophy shows why she believes this will connect with the young people in her classroom and why she is determined to continue to develop her craft:

> I think SACPs are a sure way to get high engagement and authentic learning experiences. I always catch myself thinking about how I can make the American Revolution relevant for kids. It's obvious, right, the circumstances that encourage people to challenge authority—which is a common experience in a middle schooler's life. Yet I struggle with it because while I try to make those connections during my lessons, I've also got so many other content- and skill-related ideas to address within

the same lesson. SACPs appeal to me because I think that taking the teacher out of the center of learning—away from the front of the class-room—and engaging in side-by-side learning and facilitating is a more powerful experience for kids. Not that it's less work for the teacher, but it's more meaningful for the kids.

Milli's hopefulness about finding powerful, engaging, and authentic experiences is clearly reflected in FH's newest curricular endeavor, Facing Ferguson (Facing History, 2016). Milli shared her excitement about how in the coming weeks she and like-minded teachers from the area will be getting together to deliberate about a curriculum centered on the media's represen-tations of police brutality and the targeting of young men of color. Given the epidemic of violence in the local area and around the country, Milli sees direct links from this curriculum to the lives of her students—a springboard, if you will, for other opportunities for students to name topics and issues im-portant to them. Excited to bring the curricular ideas back to her students, Milli has already met with her administration about using Facing Ferguson as an entryway for student-driven social action curriculum projects related to their own personal concerns. With the backing of FH and with the tre-mendous growth her students have exhibited through her teaching, Milli indicates that her administration is excited about this idea. Milli's enthusiasm is contagious as she is knee-deep in the planning stages of figuring out how to allow space for an emergent curriculum that can be documented well in advance and also aligns with the necessary mandates of her school. While the mandates may be frustrating at times, Milli's administration needs to be recognized and celebrated for its willingness to make spaces for teachers to engage in such approaches to teaching and learning.

In similar ways to how Milli relies heavily on FH to approach curriculum in meaningful ways that she believes will resonate with her students, Jennifer McSurley leans on curricular materials and frameworks from the organization Mikva Challenge. In the next section, readers can see how Jennifer leverages this organization's resources and reputation, along with support from her district, to help connect with her students and develop worthwhile curricu-lum with them.

STILL FINDING CRACKS:
STUDENT VOICE COMMITTEES TO ADVOCATE FOR CHANGE

Jennifer McSurley's commitment to teaching for social justice and utilizing a social action curriculum project approach, detailed in Chapter 3, is steadfast and has continued in her next teaching environment. But finding the ways to teach in the cracks has become consistently more difficult amid more pressures, more tests, and higher stakes in her new classroom. Now teaching middle schoolers in a neighborhood magnet-cluster Chicago public school, Jennifer has sought different ways to find cracks in an even more restrictive classroom context because of the constant attention and value placed on standardized achievement tests.

Like Milli in the public charter school, Jennifer looks to the help and materials of outside organizations in partnership with her school and school district to pave the way for a robust curriculum in her school. One such way that Jennifer realizes the power of looking to students' ideas to continue inverting the curriculum is through her use of a Student Voice Committee (SVC). SVCs are a component of the Action Civics curriculum materials developed in partnership with Chicago Public Schools (CPS) by the nonprofit, nonpartisan Mikva Challenge, an organization whose mission centers on promoting youth to be active, empowered citizens and on developing youth leaders (Mikva Challenge, 2013, 2014). According to the Mikva Challenge (2013) curriculum materials, "Student Voice Committees are designed to form crucial student–adult partnerships to help address the myriad of issues facing schools today. The primary goals for these councils are: 1. to improve school culture, and 2. to develop leadership skills of each youth" (p. ii).

Through a pilot project supported initially by Chicago Public Schools Department of Literacy's programs in Civic Engagement and Service Learning (which are now housed in the Department of Social Science and Civic Engagement) (Chicago Public Schools, 2015, 2016), Jennifer seized the opportunity to become her school's facilitator for an SVC. CPS had been utilizing SVCs in high schools, but appropriately determined that the concepts and ideas ought to be applied at the middle school level as well so as to create spaces for young adolescent civic engagement. CPS should be celebrated for seeking necessary outside funding to make this happen and in turn supporting this important work. In Jennifer's case, at first the SVC unfortunately was relegated to an after-school program rather than explicitly embedded in her classroom because of the constraints associated with her school context. But that did not stop the enthusiasm Jennifer or her students had for engaging in agency-oriented work through the SVC. With 15 students, the group met each Thursday afternoon after school to examine topics associated with the school climate that were important to the students.

The first issue the students decided to tackle in the past year related to their 8th-grade graduation. Breaking a longstanding school tradition, with the best of intentions in mind, a new school principal recently had made the decision to hold the graduation ceremony at a nearby private school. Up in

arms about the pronouncement and fueled by school pride, the students mo-
bilized. Jennifer drew on her past experiences with social action curriculum
projects and leaned on the framework offered via the SVC to facilitate the
efforts. The students followed a 4-step process to take action related to this
pressing issue.

> Step 1: Establish the Foundation of the Committee
> Step 2: Analyze the School Community
> Step 3: Conduct Research and Develop Solution Ideas
> Step 4: Implement Solutions and Reflect (Mikva Challenge, 2013, p. ii)

According to Jennifer, the "students extensively discussed the issue and
possible solutions as well as researched the issue, conducted student and parent surveys, spoke to teachers involved, and came up with their own presentation" to make the case for their cause of moving the graduation back to
their home turf. Whereas Jennifer utilized this Mikva/CPS framework for
the SVCs, she also made it her own by adapting it to her context and drawing
on her previous experiences as well as her strong teacher vision about ways
in which to allow students' voices to be prominent in curriculum making.
This is important because teachers do not need to follow an explicit script
when using curricular materials such as those developed by organizations like
Mikva Challenge to exploit cracks in an already-determined school curriculum. As Mikva's chief education officer and former high school social studies
teacher Jill Bass explained to me, the Mikva curricular materials are "designed
to be adapted by each and every teacher. . . . It is a palette from which teachers choose how to mix the colors."

Having been invited as a guest to witness firsthand Jennifer's students'
presentation to the school administration, it was clear to me they "mixed
their palette" with passion and, importantly, compelling research. Through a
captivating presentation in which each student participated, the young people persuasively articulated their stance, presented data slides complete with
pie charts and graphs, and took questions from school administrators. The
students were readily able to answer tough questions about their data and
backed up their arguments. Months of preparation related to an issue they
felt strongly about led the students to convince the principal to change the
graduation venue back to their school. Kudos to the administration for listening to and learning from the students!

Not only did this graduation campaign clearly lead to success for the
students on this particular issue, but it also led to more spaces for Jennifer
to open in the classroom curriculum. The SVC focused the students' energy
on other issues to tackle and, perhaps as important, according to Jennifer,

Figure 6.1. The #dontlabelme student voice committee members along with teacher Jennifer McSurley. (Photo: Sandra Henkels)

allowed her to integrate some of the work into classroom curriculum endeavors. One big effort centered on an antibullying campaign the students called "#dontlabelme" (see Figure 6.1). The young people named issues related to bullying and labeling, and set out to develop education and information on the topic. Other classrooms got involved and older kids worked with younger kids on bringing attention to this critical matter.

When questioned whether she was able to more fully integrate an SVC/social action curriculum into her daily teaching, Jennifer responded:

> I think the kids definitely felt like class time was the obvious way. I was worried about admin and how far I could push, but we asked, went forward, and I certainly didn't let the kids know I was worried. I think the point of the SVC is to build up a positive school culture and that means classroom time. I knew we had to make an attempt.

Having been invited to be a guest when the administration weighed in on the earlier graduation issue, the SVC left me with no wonder why the administration would allow additional space to engage in this kind of work embedded in the classroom curriculum, albeit with some nervousness on Jennifer's end. I saw students demonstrating tangible skills, presenting compelling artifacts, and showing knowledge acquisition and development. Jennifer concurred, commenting, "Our initial display of intelligence, prep, and seriousness really showed admin we were not playing around. The graduation project was a jumping off point to push for more and the kids definitely felt it." In addition, Jennifer remarked that the SVCs led her students to demonstrate "better behavior, more motivation, and progress with their academics."

SHACKLING TEACHERS:
(MIS)USE OF THE TYLER RATIONALE IN SCHOOLS TODAY

There is a lot to celebrate about both Milli's and Jennifer's classrooms, but both teachers are in search for more opportunities, autonomy, and the ability to allow for the curriculum to emerge from their students' ideas and concerns. This very notion of emergence in curriculum is complicated in Milli's and Jennifer's classrooms by an overreliance on a framework that often is misunderstood. This framework is commonplace in the American educational landscape, and for decades many educational initiatives have relied on it for planning, implementing, and evaluating curricular matters. Importantly, while the application of this framework affects Milli's and Jennifer's teaching, its use is much broader and farther-reaching than any one school or classroom, and thus should not be read as a critique of where Milli and Jennifer teach.

The framework has become known as the Tyler Rationale and is based on a best-selling and highly popular work of Ralph Tyler, *Basic Principles of Curriculum and Instruction*, published in 1949. In the book, Tyler "attempts to explain a rationale for viewing, analyzing and interpreting the curriculum and instructional program of an educational institution" (p. 1). Prior to laying out this rationale as a series of questions to contemplate, Tyler cautions the reader that the ideas are not a textbook or manual, but rather one way of examining curriculum and instruction as tools for educational institutions. Tyler goes as far as encouraging students of curriculum to theorize or propose other rationales to develop effective curriculum. If only Tyler's own words had been heeded by curriculum developers and educational reformers of the past 60 plus years, Milli and Jennifer and countless teacher colleagues might have the freedom and encouragement to enact a more emergent form of curriculum that is responsive to the children and the events happening in their lives.

In the 1949 book, Tyler spells out what is now called "the Tyler Rationale":

> The rationale developed here begins with identifying four fundamental questions which must be answered in developing any curriculum and plan of instruction. These are:

1. What educational purposes should the school seek to attain?
2. What educational experiences can be provided that are likely to attain these purposes?
3. How can these educational experiences be effectively organized?
4. How can we determine whether these purposes are being attained? (p. 1)

We can see these ideas in many of the present-day curricular materials: the expectation of beginning with purposes and objectives followed by activities and ending with assessment and evaluation. This is clearly evident in the ways that Milli plans and develops assessments weeks in advance via the template that her school has set and in the expectation that she will make her curricular materials available on a shared calendar with administrators. It is also a part of the dilemma that Jennifer faces at her school and explains in part why she initially had to relegate to after-school programming curriculum that is more emergent in nature. Importantly, though, Tyler's initial caution that prefaced his four fundamental questions was reiterated on the last page of his book. Tyler emphatically indicated that his rationale was not a recipe or an expectation that should be followed in lock-step fashion. Instead, he framed a rhetorical question about

> whether the sequence of steps to be followed should be the same as the order of presentation in this syllabus. The answer is clearly "No." . . . The purpose of the rationale is to give a view of the elements that are involved in a program of instruction and their necessary interrelations. The program may be improved by attacks beginning at any point, providing the resulting modifications are followed through the related elements until eventually all aspects of the curriculum have been studied and reviewed. (Tyler, 1949, p. 128)

Notably, Tyler argues that a curricular program can start at any point along the continuum of the questions in his proposal. Unfortunately, this is not a common approach in most schools or curriculum materials today. If Tyler's ideas and warning had been considered over the decades, might both Milli and Jennifer not be in the situations in which they find themselves today? Would each be able to engage with students in more emergent curricula?

As popularity of the Tyler Rationale grew in the first 25 years after it was published in book form, Tyler spoke about the *Basic Principles* and reflected on their usage in education of the day. At a curriculum theory conference in 1976 in Milwaukee, Tyler (1977) articulated the following:

> As I reviewed the earlier syllabus, I found no reason to change the basic questions it raises. What should be the educational objectives of the curriculum? What

learning experiences should be developed to enable the students to obtain the objectives? How should the learning experiences be organized to increase their cumulative effect? How should the effectiveness of the curriculum be evaluated? These are still basic and their importance has been reaffirmed by the experiences of the past quarter of a century. However, some changes of emphasis are necessary and I want to comment on two of them.

I would give much greater emphasis now to careful consideration of the implications for curriculum development of the active role of the student in the learning process. I would also give much greater emphasis to a comprehensive examination of the nonschool areas of student learning in developing curriculum. (p. 37)

As Milli and Jennifer work to connect the out-of-school lives and issues important to their students to their classroom curriculum, we should collectively reflect on the importance of the active role of students and how we can be responsive to their lives when developing curriculum. In so doing, we might recognize how evaluation of curriculum can be a means to improve instruction and build capacity among teachers and students alike, rather than being associated with comparing, rating, and more punitive motives. Together, for the sake of our students and, in turn, the teachers who seek to provide spaces and opportunities to educate them, we need to push back on the tendency of misuse or misunderstanding of the Tyler Rationale.

Taken together, Milli and Jennifer can be seen as activist teachers searching for cracks and openings to push back against an oversimplification of the Tyler Rationale enacted within the current pressures of school reform today. Both of them work within the system, clearly plan and execute amazing teaching for and with their students, and are appropriately celebrated at their respective schools for following the initiatives and expectations of their school administrators. Though both teachers are wrestling with finding ways they can be the teachers they want to be, each of them has found profound successes in her classroom, even amid what Tyler and other curriculum scholars since have cautioned against.

The use of Facing History and Ourselves and Mikva Challenge provides these teachers with concrete avenues to begin enacting their vision with their students, while satisfying the demands associated with our current environment. Teachers interested in enacting justice- and action-oriented curriculum in their classrooms, but who feel constrained by standards, accountability mandates, or other prescriptions, might consider looking to outside organizations that can help them find and exploit cracks in a seemingly more restrictive curricular environment. Given the reliance on frameworks focused on detailing objectives, planning activities, and subsequently assessing them, often in high-stakes scenarios, finding ways to reach students is more imperative than ever.

In the next chapter, I provide details on how to access the materials described in this chapter. I also point readers to additional resources from other similar organizations, including Zinn Education Project and Teaching Tolerance, as well as the organizations I relied heavily on in my own teaching: the Center for Civic Education and the Constitutional Rights Foundation Chicago. My hope is that by sharing multiple techniques for participation, suggesting outside organizations, and highlighting viable low- or no-cost resources, I may assist and guide teachers in finding openings in their own classrooms to become the teachers they want to be.

CHAPTER 7

Turning the Corner

Techniques, Resources, and Tools for Taking Action

TECHNIQUES FOR PARTICIPATION

When I was teaching in a 5th-grade classroom in Chicago, I had an out-of-the-ordinary experience. A classroom supporter who had backed my students' efforts to push the city and school district to make good on the promise for a new school building to serve their housing project community informed one of my students via email that Ralph Nader was going to be in Chicago. This classroom supporter urged the 5th-graders and me to try to get Nader involved in our cause. She was now encouraging my students to find other allies who could raise the profile of their organizing campaign. Believing Ralph Nader could do just that, she suggested that he would be impressed with the young people's efforts related to a community problem to help their neighborhood. She was right. Not only was Nader impressed by what he initially thought were efforts of high school students, but he also began writing and publishing about the students, paid the class a visit at school while on the campaign trail during his run for president, and brought additional national media attention to their immediate cause. Because of this, my 5th-grade students' organizing efforts became part of the broader conversation related to the ways in which many urban youth historically have been marginalized through inadequate schools and school resources. A more complete version of this story, and my thoughts about it, has been told elsewhere (see Schultz, 2008). What has not yet been articulated is some of the ideas I took away from my serendipitous interactions with Mr. Nader and the resources he pointed me to that might facilitate taking action.

Among the ideas discussed during our brief initial interaction, Nader suggested that I check out a book by Katherine Isaac, *Civics for Democracy: A Journey for Teachers and Students* (1992), specifically looking to a chapter that outlined different "techniques for participation." The book chronicles many different ways students have taken action related to causes that the young people found important, outlines the history of civil rights movements over the 20th century, and presents different activities students can do to engage more fully in civics. High schools all over the country purchased copies of the book when it was published in the early 1990s. But because of the frequent marginalization or absence of civics curricula in schools at that time, in practice the books often were not used as fully as they could have been. Perhaps it is now the time to share this resource again, as many state boards of education, including here in Illinois recently, are promoting service learning, civics education, and civic engagement practices. In the case of Illinois, it is referred to as the civics mandate (see, for example, Illinois's Public Act: www.ilga.gov/legislation/publicacts/fulltext.asp?Name=099-0434).

After my encounter with Nader, I got my hands on a used copy of *Civics for Democracy* and went straight to the techniques section. Struck by its accessibility and listing of different techniques, I quickly photocopied this part for my 5th-grade students. When I shared it with them to further the ways in which we were engaged in our organizing efforts and action planning, my students' initial response was that they were already doing many of the techniques outlined in the chapter. They were right. They had already developed a comprehensive action plan that they were putting into action. Challenged to name a problem in their community, the students had identified the inadequacy of their school building, which was in shameful condition. Their action plan centered on ways they could realize what they called their "perfect solution: a whole new school building." Many of the techniques detailed by Isaac were things in which they were engaged or ideas that they had intended to take on in order to build momentum related to their cause. Rather than being dissuaded by the fact that they had already thought independently about some of the techniques mentioned in the book, the students were encouraged by the reading since it affirmed that they were already taking action with purpose, and that others who had been a part of other movements before them saw merit in the various ways in which they were taking action. There was a connection between what they had been doing and what the techniques in the book detailed.

Since that time, I often have found that sharing Isaac's techniques for participation with aspiring teachers in my college classroom or with practicing teachers in schools helps them to see how they may engage with students and "turn the proverbial corner" to facilitate student action. Most of my university students as well as many young people in schools are readily able to document a problem. They have no trouble articulating an issue that needs to be remedied, solved, or obliterated. Naming the issues is often the easy part. But figuring out what to do next is where many people, both young and old, get stuck. The techniques for participation assist them in seeing how methods that other people have utilized, and that civil rights campaigns and movements have leveraged, can be applied to the issue or problem that they are trying to solve.

In her text, Isaac lists, operationalizes, and annotates different tactics, techniques, and methods that help further a cause. By highlighting ways for utilizing individual action, research, direct action, citizen lobbying, the courts, and the media via citizen access to newspapers, television, and radio, Isaac points readers to the multitude of techniques for participation in democratic and citizen action. Some of these techniques include:

- Background research
- Boycotts
- Call-in shows
- Clearinghouses
- Committee hearings
- Demonstrations and protests
- Feature stories
- Forming a citizen group
- Identifying key players
- Initiatives and referendums
- Leaflets, flyers, posters, and bulletin boards
- Letters to the editor
- News releases
- Newsletters
- Nonviolent civil disobedience
- Op-eds
- Pamphleteering
- Picketing
- Public hearings, candidate nights, film/video screenings
- Public service announcements
- Recruiting supporters
- Reports and surveys
- Right to know
- Speakers' bureaus
- Using the courts
- Whistleblowing
- Writing a bill and finding a sponsor (To see the full discussion of these techniques, refer to Isaac, 1992, pp. 157–182, or Isaac's 1997 book, *Ralph Nader's Practicing Democracy.*)

After sharing Isaac's techniques for participation and discussing the various opportunities for taking action, I challenge my university students to think about the 21st-century list of techniques that could be written. Which of the techniques in the list above are appropriate for taking action today? What is missing? What might be most effective? These questions raise issues related to whether the techniques are dated given the advent of social media and the Internet. I push students to think about this and I offer some ideas and perspectives on what more current techniques of participation may look like that might assist teachers in engaging in action-oriented, emergent curricula with their students. Often in the university classroom, my students will brainstorm ideas that resonate with them. Some of these ideas include:

- Apps
- Blogs
- Culture jamming
- Facebook
- Flashmobs
- Freedom of Information Act request (FOIA)
- Instagram
- LinkedIn
- Listservs
- Mapping
- Online surveys
- Periscope
- Photo captioning
- PhotoVoice
- Podcasts
- Pop-up stands
- Public and performance art
- RSS feeds
- Snapchat
- Twitter
- Video documentation
- Websites
- YouTube

In addition to naming the various techniques, I raise the question with university students about how the various techniques they come up with or the ones that Isaac named in her book can be utilized for covering specific topics, aligning with standards, and meeting mandates in schools, as can be seen in Figure 7.1.

Whereas I am not as concerned with aligning curriculum with standards or meeting prescriptive mandates as I am with developing emergent

Figure 7.1. Public action and techniques for participation can readily align with school subjects or mandated requirements. (Photo: Brian Schultz)

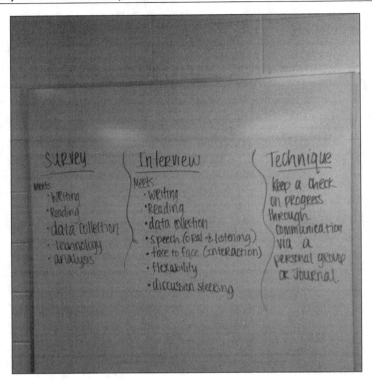

curriculum with students, I realize that many educators are teaching in contexts where the former are concerns. Instead of resisting these prescriptive situations, I want my future and practicing teachers to see how doing action-oriented curriculum and engaging with young people through techniques for participation readily can cover standards, meet expectations, and help them articulate and demonstrate specific, tangible learning occurring inside and outside of their classrooms. It is through such various techniques that teachers can highlight learning and show artifacts that illustrate deep engagement—certainly better than any worksheet or rote learning.

Many other university-based researchers have shown how different subject areas as well as project-based work can incorporate action, inquiry, civic literacy, and justice-oriented classroom activities, while also aligning with standards (see, for example, Agarwal-Rangnath, 2013; Agarwal-Rangnath, Dover, & Henning, 2016; Dover, 2015; Epstein, 2014; Gutstein & Peterson, 2013; Wolk, 2013; Zemelman, 2016). I encourage readers who need to identify such standards-based alignment for lesson or unit plans to seek out resources from teachers and scholars who have examined and documented ways in which inquiry-based social justice teaching and learning provide rich learning opportunities that also can meet such outside expectations.

ORGANIZATIONS AND THEIR RESOURCES

Whereas I promote the idea of creating curriculum by looking to students to name the issues that are important to them, and value opportunities in partnering with community-based organizations, I realize that this may not always be possible. The cracks in a classroom, school, or district may be much smaller, and thus imagining the possibilities may be harder or not possible at all. I am still hopeful.

I strongly encourage practitioners to find organizations that can support their teaching and learning efforts. This can be seen in both Chapters 4 and 6 of this book. At Dr. Pedro Albizu Campos Puerto Rican High School, teachers and administrators partnered with community-based organizations to create avenues for relevant, responsive, and action-oriented curricula to emerge from neighborhood issues. In other schools and classrooms, the partnering takes a different form: Outside educational advocacy organizations provide materials and professional development to help teachers reach their students. These kinds of educational organizations have developed curricular materials that can support teachers and students alike for doing justice-oriented, inquiry-based, and social action– or public policy–oriented work in the classroom.

Often these organizations align their materials with the Common Core State Standards or other mandates that affect teachers, schools, and districts. Many times, the organizations have a broad reach, a national reputation, and support teams for professional development or simply to answer questions that can assist teachers looking to take on such initiatives in their classrooms. Instead of having to make the case themselves, teachers can rely on some of the already-available materials, lesson plans, and other resources that these organizations provide—many free to teachers. This was clearly the case for Jennifer McSurley's work with Mikva Challenge's Student Voice Committees detailed in Chapter 6. Likewise, in that same chapter, Milli Salguero effectively leveraged resources and materials from Facing History and Ourselves. And when I was in the classroom myself, I found the materials and resources, particularly related to Project Citizen, from both the Center for Civic Education and the Constitutional Rights Foundation Chicago to be invaluable in helping to support classroom efforts.

These organizations are highlighted below, along with Teaching Tolerance, a great resource sponsored by the Southern Poverty Law Center. These are nonprofit organizations whose missions center on justice issues and civic engagement. They not only are doing good work that can help teachers get started exploring action-oriented curriculum in their classrooms, but also have aligned their materials with current standards, making those materials more readily usable for teachers seeking to integrate such approaches into their classrooms.

- Mikva Challenge (mikvachallenge.org) provides digital downloadable books on action civics, Student Voice Committees, and democracy in action. The organization has professional development opportunities for educators and hosts a practitioners' conference. The materials are Common Core State Standards–aligned.
- Center for Civic Education (civiced.org) has digital downloadable activity books for Project Citizen for middle and high school curriculum in both English and Spanish, some of which are available for free previews. This program guides and teaches participants to engage in government and public policy issues.
- Facing History and Ourselves (facinghistory.org) provides books, classroom borrowing sets, teaching strategies, lesson plans, and professional development that promote teachers in examining racism, prejudice, and anti-Semitism with their students.
- Constitutional Rights Foundation Chicago (crfc.org) provides a curriculum and professional development support for its Action-Based Communities Project, which encourages teachers to do civic engagement and public policy change work with students in their classrooms.
- Teaching Tolerance (tolerance.org) provides free classroom resources, film kits, and professional development aligned with its antibias framework. Its Perspectives for a Diverse America (perspectives.tolerance.org) platform allows teachers to create literacy-based, antibias learning plans via an online archive of questions, text collections, activities, and assessments.

Beyond the resources detailed above, some of these organizations provide just-in-time, culturally responsive curricular materials that focus on current and/or controversial events. An example of this is the professional development workshop on the Facing Ferguson curriculum that Milli Salguero attended. With materials like these, teachers have tools readily available to embed activities and classroom discussions that center the curriculum on issues students are contemplating currently.

Importantly, though, the list of organizations above is not exhaustive. There are many other educational advocacy groups, nonprofits, and community-based organizations doing great work that can be adapted for and implemented in classrooms. Other national organizations that provide strong justice-oriented curricular ideas include: Zinn Education Project (zinnedproject.org), Teaching for Change (teachingforchange.org), and Rethinking Schools (rethinkingschools.org). Similarly, the Illinois Mathematics and Science Academy (imsa.edu), High Tech High (hightechhigh.org), the Buck Institute for Education (bie.org), and the Apple-developed Challenge Based Learning (challengebasedlearning.org) offer ideas, resources, and guides to implementing project- and problem-based learning in classrooms that can readily support teachers in their quest to develop emergent curricula with students. Teachers also can draw ideas from the Google-inspired 20% Time Projects (20timeineducation.com) to find ways to integrate student interests and ideas into their classrooms. A key takeaway here is that teachers should seek out both local and national organizations that fit their needs in attempting to do emergent, project- and problem-based, and justice-oriented curriculum, or should find other educators doing this work to collaborate with or draw inspiration from in order to enact powerful, worthwhile teaching and learning. Whether or not teachers have the ability to create the spaces in which to develop curriculum in organic ways on their own with students in their classrooms, seeking allies, finding partnerships, and building relationships with individuals and groups in and out of schools are particularly critical to the success of emergent curriculum.

TOOLS RELATED TO TAKING ACTION

Whether developing curriculum alongside students from scratch, or leaning on already-available curricula from an educational advocacy organization or a nonprofit, teachers can look to some of the following web-based tools and resources to facilitate their efforts. Whenever possible, I have identified these resources with an eye toward tools that are either free or nonproprietary so that taking action with students is not cost prohibitive, particularly for teachers in underresourced schools. Many of the free resources on websites have upgrades available that often have associated costs so teachers should be mindful as they explore on their own and with students. When taking action, especially with regard to acts of culture jamming and other forms of civil disobedience, teachers and students should make sure to follow applicable laws and understand consequences before engaging in such activities. With infinite resources coming online all the time, the websites presented in

Table 7.1 are merely a starting point for teachers looking to engage in action-oriented ways with their students.

REFLECT, CONTEMPLATE, AND FIND INSPIRATION

Teachers interested in this approach to curriculum certainly can find many ways to be inspired from other people engaging in movement-making and social action projects. The ideas and tools in Table 7.1 can be possible starting points for places to experiment and experience with students. Perhaps these ideas will push teachers to think of others. Certainly in my university classes, my students and I brainstorm ways to take action and are always coming up with new and different approaches; I am continually learning new ideas or techniques from them.

Examining other examples of engagement in broad social action curriculum projects is also a means for discovering ways for taking action. By looking to people or groups who are organizing for change, who are performing culture jams or spectacles, or who are taking up a particular cause, some of my classes have been challenged to think about how to take action and, in turn, how they can support their students in doing so as well. There are many examples of such work. Some that I have shared or intend to share with students include the organizing work of the Jane Addams Hull House Museum (hullhousemuseum.org), the Street Vendor Project (streetvendor.org and turnstiletours.org), the Black Lives Matter movement (blacklivesmatter.com), as well as the racial justice work of multimedia visual artist Samuel Levi Jones (samuellevijones.com, see Figure 7.2).

Pointing students to culture jammers and those who engage in spectacle through the performance art of Reverend Billy and the Stop Shopping Choir (revbilly.com), Banksy's graffiti art (banksy.co.uk), and the documentary work of Morgan Spurlock in *Supersize Me* and *30 Days* (morganspurlock.com) has helped me articulate ways—often through hyperbole—in which action can be taken. Some educators have found success in highlighting different longtime agitators and activists like United Farm Workers leaders Cesar Chavez and Dolores Huerta and consumer advocate Ralph Nader to show how other movements mobilize people. And drawing attention to possibilities of different ways of thinking through TedTalks (ted.com) can be helpful to see the multiple approaches and techniques for engaging in various issues. Further, I have found that challenging students to connect with local community-based organizations that are working on different issues related to, for instance, housing, violence, healthy food access, LGBTQ rights, or education shows them the many facets and the multiplicity of approaches to taking action.

Table 7.1. Classroom tools and resources for taking action.

Technique	Topics	Web Address	Explanation
Letters, Emails, Contacting Legislators	Finding Your Legislators	openstates.org/find_your_legislator	enter your address to determine your local legislators
FOIA	How to File a FOIA Request	citizen.org/Page.aspx-?pid=458	how-to guide for completing a Freedom of Information Act (FOIA) request
Petitions	Online Petition Websites	change.org thepetitionsite.com ipetitions.com	platforms for creating free online petitions
Op-Ed	The Op-Ed Project	theopedproject.org	resources section that suggests basic structure, tips, and how to pitch op-eds
Surveys and Forms	Online Survey Tools	surveymonkey.com google.com/forms	develop, distribute, and analyze free online surveys
Demographics and Mapping	Mapping Tools	google.com/mapmaker google.com/earth scribblemaps.com socialexplorer.com/explore/maps	create and share free maps in various formats, or explore demographic data through maps
Websites	Website Development Platforms	weebly.com wix.com google.com/sites google.com/webdesigner	create free websites
Flyers, Leaflets, Posters and Documents	Document Creator	canva.com	create and share free flyers, posters, social media materials, ads, postcards, and other documents
Media Literacy	Media Literacy Educator Resources	medialit.org/educator-resources	resources for teaching media literacy
Blog	Blogging Platforms	wordpress.com blogger.com	create a free blog
Protests and Demonstrations	Know Your Rights	aclu.org/know-your-rights/what-do-if-your-rights-are-violated-demonstration-or-protest wikihow.com/Protest	guides to participating in free speech, protests, and demonstrations

Table 7.1. Continued.

Technique	Topics	Web Address	Explanation
Performance Art	How to Organize a Flashmob	wikihow.com/Organize-a-Flash-Mob blog.hubspot.com/blog/tabid/6307/bid/28095/A-Step-by-Step-Guide-to-Planning-an-AWESOME-Flash-Mob.aspx#sm.0001hx-4as8m71cwisy113w9x-hchui	step-by-step instructions for creating a flashmob
PhotoVoice	PhotoVoice Manual for Participatory Photography	photovoice.org/photo-voice-manual	guide for designing participatory photography and digital storytelling projects
Video Documentation	Making Documentaries: A Step-by-Step Guide	desktop-documentaries.com/making-documentaries.html	steps, resources, and tips for making video documentaries
Apps	Build an App	ibuildapp.com appypie.com	design and develop a mobile app using available templates
Podcast	How to Make a Podcast	digitaltrends.com/how-to/how-to-make-a-podcast audacityteam.org alex.state.al.us/show-page.php?lnk=teacher-zonedircommentpod-castdircommentpodcast-tools	step-by-step guide to making a podcast, and free audio editor and recorder
Spoken Word	Become a Slam Poet	ed.ted.com/lessons/become-a-slam-poet-in-five-steps-gayle-danley youngchicagoauthors.org/ltab-2	how-to video from TED-Ed and Young Chicago Authors Louder Than a Bomb Youth Poetry Slam
Letters to the Editor	Writing Effective Letters to the Editor	reclaimdemocracy.org/effective_letters_editor	guide for writing letters to the editor
Culture Jamming	How to Culture Jam	wikihow.com/Culture-Jam	step-by-step ways to culture jam
GIFs	Create and Share GIFS	giphy.com	search, discover, share, and create animated GIFs

Figure 7.2. 48 Portraits (underexposed). 2012. Inkjet prints on recycled encyclopedia paper. With his provocative art, Samuel Levi Jones challenges people to consider the racial justice implications of who is and is not represented in supposedly "objective" texts such as encyclopedias. (Photo: Samuel Levi Jones)

* * *

The techniques, resources, and tools in this chapter, coupled with the examples from practitioners in the previous chapters, can be read as suggestions or prompts for teachers to turn the proverbial corner for enacting action-focused and student-centered curriculum in their classrooms. My hope is that educators find the necessary openings, seek out opportunities, and exploit cracks within our rigid educational policies to make good on my invitation to do something different in schools. In so doing, practitioners have the deep potential to create relevant and responsive teaching, honor what students name as worthwhile, develop the capacity for student agency, and satisfy outside mandates. Working alongside their students, these educators can develop powerful curriculum and learning that has the promise to motivate, engage, and inspire students.

Afterword

This book is an invitation—an invitation to rethink teaching from top to bottom, to dive into classroom life as a passionate adventure in discovery and surprise, and to explore an approach to teaching that's grounded first and foremost in the lives and experiences of children. I hope the invitation was accepted, and that the voyage thus far has been challenging and inspiring, that it's allowed you to dream a bit beyond the boundaries of received wisdom, and that you've been able to turn a few of your wildest reflections into tentative teaching experiments. You've no doubt discovered that action-oriented, child-centered teaching not only engages and motivates students, it enlivens and fires teachers with zest and zeal as well.

Every educational leader and every school claims to want students and graduates who are independent learners and critical thinkers, productive people and thoughtful, caring citizens. But too many schools fail dismally when it comes to delivering on their own lofty mission statements—they build a school experience that is hierarchical and hyper-individualistic, where "learning" is externally motivated and constantly competitive. They ignore everything we know about authentic learning: that learning and living are twins, for example, and that learning starts naturally at birth with no outside rewards or punishments needed to get busy on an endless journey to know and to be; that curiosity, agency, and imagination are our common human heritage; and that the best parents and teachers nurture what's already there—in abundance.

Obsessions with obedience, standardization, conformity, and control characterize too many classrooms—especially in schools attended by the descendants of enslaved people, immigrant children from poor countries, and First Nations youth. Knowing and accepting one's place on the grand pyramid of winners and losers becomes the core lesson. These schools develop elaborate schemes for managing the unruly mob, and they turn on the familiar technologies of constraint—ID cards, transparent backpacks, uniform dress codes, cameras, armed guards, metal detectors, and random searches. The knotted system of rules, the exhaustive machinery of schedules and surveillance, the prison architecture, the laborious programs of regulating, indoctrinating, inspecting, disciplining, censuring, correcting, counting, appraising, assessing and judging, testing and grading—all of it makes these places feel like institutions of punishment rather than sites of enlightenment and liberation, places to recover from rather than experiences to carry forward.

When school is geared to the absorption of facts, learning becomes exclusively and exhaustively selfish, and there is no obvious social motive for it. When the measure of success is competitive, people are turned against one another and every difference becomes a score for somebody and a deficit for someone else. Getting ahead of others is the first goal, and mutual assistance, which can be so entirely natural in other human relations, is severely restricted or banned.

Brian Schultz documents and promotes practices that can become a powerful antidote to all that. Exploring, experimenting, questioning, researching, and undertaking active work in the community becomes the order of the day, and working collaboratively, even helping others, is neither cheating nor a form of charity. A spirit of open communication, interchange, and analysis becomes a common and authentic expression of learning in these places, and there is a natural disorder as there is in any busy workshop. But there is also a sense of joy, and a deeper discipline at work, the discipline of getting things done collectively and learning *from* rather than *about* life. We see clearly in the teaching documented here that education at its best is always generative—in a way that training, for example, never can be—and that sharing knowledge, information, and discoveries with others diminishes nothing for ourselves.

Free people, including free teachers and free students, must learn to refuse obedience and conformity in favor of liberating dispositions of mind: initiative, questioning, courage, audacity, imagination, creativity, inventiveness, and empathy. These qualities cannot be delivered in top-down ways, but must be modeled and nourished, encouraged and defended, and mostly practiced again and again and again.

Free students are major actors in constructing their own educations, not simply objects of a regime of discipline and punish; they demand that education becomes decoupled from the inadequate and illegitimate "meritocracy model" and that the public good is understood more fundamentally. Instead of schooling-as-credentialing, sorting, gate-keeping, and controlling, education for freedom enables all students to become smarter and more aware, more capable of negotiating our shared and complex world, more able to work effectively in community and across communities. This requires cour-age—from teachers, families, communities, and students—to build alterna-tive and insurgent classrooms, schools, and community spaces focused on what we know we need rather than what we are told we must endure.

—William Ayers

References

Agarwal-Rangnath, R. (2013). *Social studies, literacy, and social justice in the common core classroom: A guide for teachers.* New York, NY: Teachers College Press.

Agarwal-Rangnath, R., Dover, A. G., & Henning, N. (2016). *Preparing to teach social studies for social justice: Becoming a renegade.* New York, NY: Teachers College Press.

Antrop-González, R. (2006). Toward the school as sanctuary concept in multicultural small school urban education: Implications for small high school reform. *Curriculum Inquiry, 36*(3), 273–301.

Antrop-González, R. (2011). *Schools as radical sanctuaries: Decolonizing urban education through the eyes of youth of color and their teachers.* Charlotte, NC: Information Age.

Ayers, W. (2004). *Teaching toward freedom: Moral commitment and ethical action in the classroom.* Boston, MA: Beacon Press.

Ayers, W. (2011). *To teach: The journey of a teacher* (3rd ed.). New York, NY: Teachers College Press.

Ayers, W. (2016). *Teaching with conscience in an imperfect world: An invitation.* New York, NY: Teachers College Press.

Beane, J. A. (1993). *A middle school curriculum: From rhetoric to reality* (2nd ed.). Westerville, OH: National Middle School Association.

Beane, J. A. (1998). *Curriculum integration: Designing the core of democratic education.* New York, NY: Teachers College Press.

Beane, J. (2005). *A reason to teach: Creating classrooms of dignity and hope.* Portsmouth, NH: Heinemann.

Chicago Public Schools. (2015). Department of Literacy: Civic Engagement and Service Learning. Retrieved from www.cps.edu/Pages/TL_CivicEngagement.aspx

Chicago Public Schools. (2016). Department of Social Science and Civic Engagement. Retrieved from www.cps.edu/ServiceLearning/Pages/ServiceLearning.aspx

Clandinin, D. J., & Connelly, F. M. (2000). *Narrative inquiry: Experience and story in qualitative research.* San Francisco, CA: Jossey-Bass.

Cremin, L. (1961). *The transformation of the school: Progressivism in American education 1876–1957.* New York, NY: Knopf.

Darling-Hammond, L., Ancess, J., & Falk, B. (Eds.). (1995). *Authentic assessment in action: Studies of schools and students at work.* New York, NY: Teachers College Press.

Dewey, J. (1907). *The school and society.* Chicago, IL: University of Chicago Press.

Dewey, J. (1916). *Democracy and education: An introduction to the philosophy of education.* New York, NY: Free Press.

Dewey, J. (1933, April 23). Dewey outlines utopian schools. *New York Times.*

Dewey, J. (1938). *Experience and education.* New York, NY: Macmillan.

Dover, A. G. (2015). Teaching for social justice and the common core: Justice-oriented curriculum for language arts and literacy. *Journal of Adolescent and Adult Literacy, 59*(5), 517–527.

Duncan, A. (2013, June 25). *Duncan pushes back on attacks on common core standards.* U.S. Department of Education. Retrieved from www.ed.gov/news/speeches/duncan-pushes-back-attacks-common-core-standards

Duncan-Andrade, J. (2009). Note to educators: Hope required when growing roses in concrete. *Harvard Educational Review, 79*(2), 181–194.

Epstein, S. E. (2014). *Teaching civic literacy projects: Student engagement with social problems.* New York, NY: Teachers College Press.

Facing History and Ourselves. (2016). Facing Ferguson: News literacy in a digital age. Retrieved from www.facinghistory.org/resource-library/facing-ferguson-news-literacy-digital-age

Flores-González, N. (2001). Paseo boricua: Claiming a Puerto Rican space in Chicago. *Centro Journal, 23*(2), 7–23.

Flores-González, N. (2002). *School kids/Street kids: Identity development in Latino students.* New York, NY: Teachers College Press.

Freire, P. (2000). *Pedagogy of the oppressed* (30th Anniversary ed.). New York, NY: Continuum. (Original work published 1970)

Greene, M. (1986). In search of a critical pedagogy. *Harvard Educational Review, 56*(4), 427–442.

Gutstein, E., & Peterson, R. (Eds.). (2013). *Rethinking mathematics: Teaching social justice by the numbers* (2nd ed.). Milwaukee, WI: Rethinking Schools.

Hess, D. (2009). *Controversy in the classroom: The democratic power of discussion.* New York, NY: Routledge.

Hopkins, L. T. (1954). *The emerging self in school and home.* New York: Harper & Brothers.

Illinois Mathematics and Science Academy. (2012). *PBL tool kit.* Aurora, IL: Author.

Irizarry, J., & Antrop-González, R. (2007). RicanStructing the discourse and promoting school success: Extending a theory of culturally responsive pedagogy for Diasporicans. *Centro Journal, 29*(2), 37–59.

Isaac, K. (1992). *Civics for democracy: A journey for teachers and students.* Washington, DC: Center for Study of Responsive Law and Essential Information.

Isaac, K. (1997). *Ralph Nader's practicing democracy: A guide to student action.* New York, NY: St. Martin's Press.

Janesick, V. (2006). *Authentic assessment.* New York, NY: Peter Lang.

Johnson, L. R. (2008). A re-storying framework: The intersection of community and family narratives in Puerto Rican Chicago. *Thresholds in Education, 34*(1), 41–47.

Johnson, L. R. (2009). Challenging best practices in family literacy and parent education programs: The development and enactment of mothering knowledge among Puerto Rican and Latina mothers in Chicago. *Anthropology & Education Quarterly, 40*(3), 257–276.

Kanigel, R. (1997). *The one best way: Frederick Winslow Taylor and the enigma of efficiency.* New York, NY: Viking Penguin.

Knoester, M. (2012). *Democratic education in practice: Inside the Mission Hill School.* New York, NY: Teachers College Press.

Ladson-Billings, G. (1995). But that's just good teaching: The case for culturally relevant pedagogy. *Theory into Practice, 34*(3), 159–165.

Ladson-Billings, G. (2009). *The dreamkeepers: Successful teachers of African American children* (2nd ed.). San Francisco, CA: Jossey-Bass.

Larmer, J., & Mergendoller, J. (2010). Seven essentials for project-based learning. *Educational Leadership, 68*(1), 34–37.

Little, T., & Ellison, K. (2015). *Loving learning: How progressive education can save America's schools.* New York, NY: Norton.

Mikva Challenge. (2013). *Student voice committees curriculum.* Chicago, IL: Author.

Mikva Challenge. (2014). *Issues to action curriculum.* Chicago, IL: Author.

Noguera, P. (2003). *City schools and the American dream: Reclaiming the promise of public education.* New York, NY: Teachers College Press.

Noguera, P. (2008). *The trouble with black boys . . . and other reflections on race, equity, and the future of public education.* San Francisco, CA: Jossey-Bass.

Oakes, J., Lipton, M., Anderson, L., & Stillman, J. (2012). *Teaching to change the world* (4th ed.). Boulder, CO: Paradigm.

Paley, V. (2005). *A child's work.* Chicago, IL: University of Chicago Press.

Progressive Education Network. (2016). Principles in practice: Progressive education & racial justice. Retrieved from www.progressiveeducationnetwork.org/progressive-education-and-racial-justice/

Ryan, D. (2017). What makes The Children's School unique? Retrieved from www.thechildrensschool.info

Sahlberg, P. (2014). *Finnish lessons 2.0: What can the world learn from educational change in Finland?* New York, NY: Teachers College Press.

Schubert, W. H. (1991). Teacher lore: A basis for understanding praxis. In C. Witherall & N. Noddings (Eds.), *Stories lives tell* (pp. 207–233). New York, NY: Teachers College Press.

Schubert, W. H. (1997). *Curriculum: Perspective, paradigm, and possibility.* Upper Saddle River, NJ: Prentice-Hall. (Original work published 1986)

Schubert, W. H. (2006). Teaching John Dewey as a Utopian pragmatist while learning from my students. *Education and Culture, 22*(1), 78–83.

Schubert, W. H. (2009a). *Love, justice, and education: John Dewey and the Utopians.* Charlotte, NC: Information Age.

Schubert, W. H. (2009b). What is worthwhile: From knowing and needing to being and sharing? *Journal of Curriculum and Pedagogy, 6*(1), 21–39.

Schubert, W. H. (2012, April). Progressive education: Its deeper meaning. *VOICE, 4*.

Schultz, B. D. (2008). *Spectacular things happen along the way: Lessons from an urban classroom.* New York, NY: Teachers College Press.

Schultz, B. D. (Ed.). (2011). *Listening to and learning from students: Possibilities for teaching, learning, and curriculum.* Charlotte, NC: Information Age.

Taylor, F. W. (1911). *The principles of scientific management.* New York, NY: Harper & Row. Retrieved from www.gutenberg.org/cache/epub/6435/pg6435-images.html

Tozer, S., & Senese, G. (2012). *School and society: Historical and contemporary perspectives* (7th ed.). New York, NY: McGraw-Hill.

Tyler, R. W. (1949). *Basic principles of curriculum and instruction.* Chicago, IL: University of Chicago Press.

Tyler, R. W. (1977). Desirable content for a curriculum development syllabus today. In A. Molnar & J. Zahorik (Eds.), *Curriculum theory* (pp. 36–44). Washington, DC: Association for Supervision and Curriculum Development.

Vevea, B. (2015, October 2). Admitting dropouts were miscounted, Chicago lowers graduation rates. Retrieved from www.npr.org/sections/ed/2015/10/02/445152363/admitting-dropouts-were-miscounted-chicago-lowers-graduation-rates

Wainer, H. (2011). *Uneducated guesses: Using evidence to uncover misguided education policies.* Princeton, NJ: Princeton University Press.

Westheimer, J., & Kahne, J. (2004). What kind of citizen? The politics of educating for democracy. *American Educational Research Journal, 41*(2), 237–269.

Wolk, S. (2013). *Caring hearts and critical minds: Literature, inquiry, and social responsibility.* Portland, ME: Stenhouse.

Zemelman, S. (2016). *From inquiry to action: Civic engagement with project-based learning in all content areas.* Portsmouth, NH: Heinemann.

Index

About the Author

Brian D. Schultz is Bernard J. Brommel Distinguished Research Professor and Chairperson of the Department of Educational Inquiry and Curriculum Studies at Northeastern Illinois University in Chicago. Brian's teaching and research focus on developing democratic and progressive education-based classrooms. At Northeastern, Brian has received Excellence Awards in Teaching and Research, and has been recognized by the American Educational Research Association (AERA) with Early Career Awards in both Narrative Research and Critical Issues in Curriculum & Cultural Studies.

Brian's book, *Spectacular Things Happen Along the Way: Lessons from an Urban Classroom* (Teachers College Press, 2008), received an American Educational Studies Association (AESA) Critics' Choice Book Award, and an AERA Outstanding Book Award in Curriculum Studies. In addition, he has edited *Listening to and Learning from Students: Possibilities for Teaching, Learning, and Curriculum* (Information Age Publishing, 2011), which received a Society of Professors of Education (SPE) Book Award, and coedited *Guide to Curriculum in Education* (SAGE, 2015), which received an AESA Critics' Choice Book Award and a SPE Book Award; *Grow Your Own Teachers: Grassroots Change for Teacher Education* (Teachers College Press, 2011); *Handbook of Public Pedagogy: Education and Learning Beyond Schooling* (Routledge, 2010); and *Articulation of Curriculum and Pedagogy for Just Society: Advocacy, Artistry, and Activism* (Educator's International Press, 2007).

Brian lives with his family just outside of Chicago.